AMERICAN POLITICAL, ECONOMIC, AND SECURITY ISSUES

PRIVATE ACTIVITY, TAX-EXEMPT AND TAX CREDIT BONDS

AMERICAN POLITICAL, ECONOMIC, AND SECURITY ISSUES

Additional books in this series can be found on Nova's website under the Series tab.

Additional E-books in this series can be found on Nova's website under the E-books tab.

GOVERNMENT PROCEDURES AND OPERATIONS

Additional books in this series can be found on Nova's website under the Series tab.

Additional E-books in this series can be found on Nova's website under the E-books tab.

AMERICAN POLITICAL, ECONOMIC, AND SECURITY ISSUES

PRIVATE ACTIVITY, TAX-EXEMPT AND TAX CREDIT BONDS

FREDRICK KJELLSON
EDITOR

Nova Science Publishers, Inc.
New York

For permission to use material from this book please contact us:
Telephone 631-231-7269; Fax 631-231-8175
Web Site: http://www.novapublishers.com

Additional color graphics may be available in the e-book version of this book.

Library of Congress Cataloging-in-Publication Data

Private activity, tax-exempt and tax credit bonds / editor, Fredrick Kjellson.
p. cm.
Includes index.
ISBN 978-1-61470-227-6 (softcover)
1. Government securities--United States. 2. Bonds--United States. 3. Municipal bonds--United States. 4. State bonds--United States. I. Kjellson, Fredrick.
HG4936.P75 2011
332.63'23--dc23

2011022219

Published by Nova Science Publishers, Inc. † New York

CONTENTS

PREFACE

The federal tax code classifies state and local bonds as either governmental bonds or private activity bonds. Governmental bonds are for projects that benefit the general public, and private activity bonds are for projects that primarily benefit private entities. Typically, the interest earned by holders of these bonds is exempt from federal income taxes. The federal tax code allows state and local governments to use tax-exempt bonds to finance certain projects that would be considered private activities. The private activities that can be financed with tax-exempt bonds are called "qualified private activities." This book provides background information on the economic rationale for the federal limitation on tax-exempt bonds for private activities and explains the rules governing qualified private activity bonds.

Chapter 1- The federal tax code classifies state and local bonds as either governmental bonds or private activity bonds. Governmental bonds are for projects that benefit the general public, and private activity bonds are for projects that primarily benefit private entities. Typically, the interest earned by holders of these bonds is exempt from federal income taxes.

The federal tax code allows state and local governments to use tax-exempt bonds to finance certain projects that would be considered private activities. The private activities that can be financed with tax-exempt bonds are called "qualified private activities." Congress uses an annual state volume cap to limit the amount of tax-exempt bond financing generally and restricts the types of qualified private activities that would qualify for tax-exempt financing to selected projects defined in the tax code.

Chapter 2- State and local governments often issue debt instruments in exchange for the use of individuals' and businesses' savings. This debt obligates state and local governments to make interest payments for the use of these savings and to repay, at some time in the future, the amount borrowed.

State and local governments finance capital facilities with debt rather than out of current tax revenue in order to match the time pattern of benefits from these capital facilities with the time pattern of tax payments.

Chapter 3- This report provides information about state and local government debt. State and local governments often issue debt instruments in exchange for the use of individuals' and businesses' savings. This debt obligates state and local governments to make interest payments for the use of these savings and to repay, at some time in the future, the amount borrowed. State and local governments finance capital facilities with debt rather than out of current tax revenue in order to match the time pattern of benefits from these capital facilities with the time pattern of tax payments.

Chapter 4- Almost all state and local governments sell bonds to finance public projects and certain qualified private activities. Most of the bonds issued are tax-exempt bonds because the interest payments are not included in the bondholder's (purchaser's) federal taxable income. In contrast, Tax Credit Bonds (TCBs) are a type of bond that offers the holder or the issuer a federal tax credit instead of interest. This report explains the tax credit mechanism and describes the market for the bonds.

There are a variety of TCBs. Qualified zone academy bonds (QZABs), which were the first tax credit bonds, were introduced as part of the Taxpayer Relief Act of 1997 (P.L. 105-34) and were introduced in 1998. Clean renewable energy bonds (CREBs) were created by the Energy Policy Act of 2005 (P.L. 109-58) and "new" CREBs by the Emergency Economic Stabilization Act of 2008 (P.L. 110-343). Gulf tax credit bonds (GTCBs) were created by the Gulf Opportunity Zone Act of 2005 (P.L. 109-135). Authority to issue GTCBs has expired. Qualified forestry conservation bonds (QFCBs) were created by the Food, Conservation, and Energy Act of 2008 (P.L. 110-246). Qualified energy conservation bonds (QECBs) and Midwest Disaster Bonds (MWDBs) were created by the Emergency Economic Stabilization Act of 2008 (P.L. 110-343).

In: Private Activity, Tax-Exempt and Tax Credit… ISBN: 978-1-61470-227-6
Editor: Fredrick Kjellson

Chapter 1

PRIVATE ACTIVITY BONDS: AN INTRODUCTION

Steven Maguire

SUMMARY

The federal tax code classifies state and local bonds as either governmental bonds or private activity bonds. Governmental bonds are for projects that benefit the general public, and private activity bonds are for projects that primarily benefit private entities. Typically, the interest earned by holders of these bonds is exempt from federal income taxes.

The federal tax code allows state and local governments to use tax-exempt bonds to finance certain projects that would be considered private activities. The private activities that can be financed with tax-exempt bonds are called "qualified private activities." Congress uses an annual state volume cap to limit the amount of tax-exempt bond financing generally and restricts the types of qualified private activities that would qualify for tax-exempt financing to selected projects defined in the tax code.

This report provides background information on the economic rationale for the federal limitation on tax-exempt bonds for private activities. In addition, this report explains the rules governing qualified private activity bonds, describes the federal limitations on private activity bonds, lists the qualified private activities, and reports each state's private activity bond volume cap.

Since private activity bonds were defined in 1968, the number of eligible private activities has been gradually increased from 12 activities to 22. The state volume capacity limit has increased from $150 million and $50 per capita in 1986 to the greater of $273.775 million or $90 per capita in 2010. Because of the $273 .775 million floor, many smaller states (21 states and the District of Columbia) are allowed to issue relatively more private activity bonds (based on the level of state personal income) than larger states (29 states). Also, more recent additions to the list of qualified activities have been exempt from a state-by-state cap and subject to a national aggregate cap.

OVERVIEW AND ISSUES FOR CONGRESS

State and local governments issue debt for most large public capital projects such as new schools, public buildings, and roads. On occasion, state and local governments will issue debt for projects whose purpose is less public in nature, such as privately owned and operated multifamily residential housing. Nevertheless, these projects are often afforded the same tax privilege as debt issued for strictly government owned and operated projects. Congress limits the use of tax-exempt bonds for private activities because of concern about the overuse of tax-exempt, private activity bonds. The tax-exempt bonds issued for qualified private activities are limited by the type of activity financed and the volume of debt used for such activities.

Overview

The federal tax code classifies state and local government bonds as either governmental bonds or private activity bonds. Generally, the interest on state and local governmental bonds is exempt from taxation whereas the interest on private activity bonds is not tax-exempt.[1] However, the federal tax code allows state and local governments to use tax-exempt bonds to finance certain projects that would otherwise be classified as private activities.[2] The private activities that can be financed with tax-exempt bonds are called "qualified private activities."[3]

The current tax exemption for qualified private activities has evolved over time. Two events, however, critically shaped the current treatment of private activity bonds. First, in 1968, Congress passed the Revenue and Expenditure Control Act of 1968 (P.L. 90-364) which established the basis for the current definition of private activity bonds. Second, after persistent challenges to the right of the federal government to restrict state and local government debt following the 1968 Act, the Supreme Court agreed to hear a case in 1988 that changed the nature of the federal tax treatment of state and local government debt. In that case, the state of South Carolina challenged the Tax Equity and Fiscal Responsibility Act of 1982 (P.L. 97-248). The 1982 Act required that state and local government tax-exempt debt must be registered.[4] The registration requirement was viewed by the states, South Carolina in particular, as an unconstitutional intrusion on the ability of states to issue debt. The Supreme Court held that the registration requirement for non-federal government debt, though federally tax-exempt, was constitutional. In somewhat of a surprise to observers at the time, the Court went beyond the registration ruling and also held the following:

> The owners of state [and local] bonds have no constitutional entitlement not to pay taxes on income they earn from the bonds, and states have no constitutional entitlement to issue bonds paying lower interest rates than other issuers.[5]

The ruling confirmed that Congress can restrict issuance of state and local tax-exempt debt and could even rescind the tax-exemption altogether.[6] Nevertheless, outright repeal of the tax-exemption is unlikely. Instead, Congress has used legislative action to modify the existing rules and definitions governing tax-exempt bonds for private activities. Generally, Congress limits the *amount* of tax-exempt debt that can be used for private-activities and restricts the *type* of private activities that can be financed with tax-exempt bonds. Congress can, and does, encourage selected private activities by exempting the activity from the volume cap or by allowing tax-exempt financing for the private activity.

Issues for Congress

As noted above, Congress uses two primary means to restrain the use of state and local debt for private activities: an annual state volume limit (or separate national aggregate limit) and restrictions on the type of qualified private activities. The private activity bond volume limit, which originated in the Deficit Reduction Act of 1984 (P.L. 98-369), was implemented because "Congress was extremely concerned with the volume of tax-exempt bonds used to finance private activities."[7] The limit and the list of qualified activities were both modified again under the Tax Reform Act of 1986 (TRA 1986, P.L. 99-5 14). At the time of the TRA 1986 modifications, the Joint Committee on Taxation identified the following specific concerns about tax-exempt bonds issued for private activities:[8]

- the bonds represent "an inefficient allocation of capital";
- the bonds "increase the cost of financing traditional governmental activities";
- the bonds allow "higher-income persons to avoid taxes by means of tax-exempt investments"; and
- the bonds contribute to "mounting [federal] revenue losses."

The inefficient allocation of capital arises from the economic fact that additional investment in tax-favored private activities will necessarily come from investment in other public projects. For example, if bonds issued for mass commuting facilities did not receive special tax treatment, some portion of the bond funds could be used for other government projects such as schools or other public infrastructure.

The greater volume of tax-exempt private activity bonds then leads to the second Joint Committee on Taxation concern listed above, higher cost of financing traditional government activities. Investors have limited resources, thus, when the supply of tax-exempt bond investments increases, issuers must raise interest rates to lure them into investing in existing government activities. In economic terms, issuers raising interest rates to attract investors is analogous to a retailer lowering prices to attract customers. The higher interest rates make borrowing more expensive for issuers.

The final two points are less important from an economic efficiency perspective but do cause some to question the efficacy of using tax-exempt bonds to deliver a federal subsidy. Tax-exempt interest is worth more to taxpayers in higher brackets, thus, the tax benefit flows to higher income taxpayers, which leads to a less progressive income tax regime.

The revenue loss generated by tax-exempt bonds also expands the deficit (or shrinks the surplus). A persistent budget deficit ultimately leads to generally higher interest rates as the government competes with private entities for scarce investment dollars. Higher interest rates further increase the cost of all debt-financed state and local government projects.

Supporters of tax-exempt bonds for private activities counter that the benefit from tax-exempt bonds exceeds both the explicit (the revenue loss) and implicit (the inefficient allocation of capital) costs of the tax-exemption.

The debate surrounding use of tax-exempt bonds will continue well beyond the current Congress. Proponents and opponents of tax-exempt bonds generally, and private activity bonds specifically, both explore methods of modifying the rules for private activity bonds to advance their respective positions. Because the rules and definitions for private activity bonds are complex, uncertainty about the potential effects of the proposed modifications to those rules is common. This report will not attempt to either justify or criticize the existence of or use of tax-exempt private activity bonds.[9] Instead, the report provides a brief review of bond fundamentals and a more detailed examination of the rules and definitions surrounding private activity bonds to help clarify the impact of the of those modifications.

FUNDAMENTALS OF PRIVATE ACTIVITY BONDS

Interest Rates on Tax-Exempt vs. Taxable Bonds

Tax-exempt bonds for governmental purposes and for qualified private activities are special because, unlike corporate bonds or U.S. Treasury bonds, the bond buyer does not have to include the interest income from the bond in federal gross taxable income.[10] The bond buyer is willing to accept a lower interest rate because the interest income is not subject to federal income taxes. The lower interest rate arising from the tax-exempt status subsidizes state and local investment in capital projects. For example, if the taxable bond interest rate is 7.00%, the after-tax return for a taxpayer in the 35% income tax bracket who buys a taxable bond is 4.55%.[11] Thus, a tax-exempt bond that offers a 4.5 5% interest rate would be just as attractive to the investor as the taxable bond, all else equal.[12] Researchers can derive an implied marginal tax rate based on current market data for taxable and tax-exempt debt.

Interest Rate Spread

The "interest rate spread" is the difference between the interest rate on tax-exempt bonds and some other taxable bond. **Table 1** below compares tax-exempt bonds to high-grade corporate bonds over the last 30 years.[13] The difference between the two interest rates is smaller empirically than the previous example because a large share of tax-exempt bond buyers are below the 35% marginal income tax bracket. Individuals in income tax brackets below 35% would require a higher tax-exempt bond interest rate because lower tax rates mean less tax savings from tax- exempt bonds.[14] The lower tax bracket taxpayers bid up the tax-exempt bond interest rate closer to the taxable bond interest rate. Generally, the two rates move in tandem, with the taxable corporate bond interest rate always higher than the tax-exempt municipal bond interest rate.[15]

In December of 2008, during unprecedented turmoil in financial markets and the economy, the average high-grade corporate bond rate was 5.05% and the average high-grade municipal (tax- exempt) bond rate was 5.56%.[16] The lower interest rates for taxable corporate bonds than for tax- exempt bonds in December 2008 was a short-lived phenomena that can be traced to the interaction of at least two factors. First, the Federal Reserve Bank (Fed) was injecting as much liquidity into the economy as possible, setting interest rates at their lowest level ever.[17] This tended to keep market interest rates on taxable debt low. Second, state and local governments were facing significant fiscal stress and the bond market reacted by requiring a risk premium on its debt. The risk premium means a higher interest rate for municipal debt. In addition, the municipal bond insurance market collapsed, further elevating the perceived risk of municipal bonds. Since then, the spread has moved closer to historical levels with tax-exempt bond interest rates at 3.86% and taxable bonds at 4.45% as of September 2, 2010. The ratio of tax-exempt debt to taxable debt is still very high at 0.87.

Table 1. Yield on Tax-Exempt and Corporate Bonds, the Yield Spread, and the Yield Ratio: 1980 to September 2010

Year	High Grade Tax-Exempt Yield (%)	AAA Corporate Yield(%)	Yield Spread (%)	Yield Ratio (tax-exempt/ corporate)
1980	8.51	11.94	3.43	0.71
1981	11.23	14.17	2.94	0.79
1982	11.57	13.79	2.22	0.84
1983	9.47	12.04	2.57	0.79
1984	10.15	12.71	2.56	0.80
1985	9.18	11.37	2.19	0.81
1986	7.38	9.02	1.64	0.82
1987	7.73	9.38	1.65	0.82

Year	High Grade Tax-Exempt Yield (%)	AAA Corporate Yield(%)	Yield Spread (%)	Yield Ratio (tax-exempt/ corporate)
1988	7.76	9.71	1.95	0.80
1989	7.24	9.26	2.02	0.78
1990	7.25	9.32	2.07	0.78
1991	6.89	8.77	1.88	0.79
1992	6.41	8.14	1.73	0.79
1993	5.63	7.22	1.59	0.78
1994	6.19	7.96	1.77	0.78
1995	5.95	7.59	1.64	0.78
1996	5.75	7.37	1.62	0.78
1997	5.55	7.26	1.71	0.76
1998	5.12	6.53	1.41	0.78
1999	5.43	7.04	1.61	0.77
2000	5.77	7.62	1.85	0.76
2001	5.19	7.08	1.89	0.73
2002	5.05	6.49	1.44	0.78
2003	4.73	5.67	0.94	0.83
2004	4.63	5.63	1.00	0.82
2005	4.29	5.24	0.95	0.82
2006	4.42	5.59	1.17	0.79
2007	4.42	5.56	1.14	0.79
2008	4.80	5.63	0.83	0.85
2009	4.64	5.31	0.67	0.87
2010, September 2	3.86	4.45	0.59	0.87

Source: Council of Economic Advisors, *Economic Report of the President*, February 2010, Table B-73, and Federal Reserve Board, "Table H. 15: Selected Interest Rates, Historical Data," available at http://www.federalreserve.gov/releases/h15/data.htm, visited September10, 2010.

Tax-Exempt Bonds and the Alternative Minimum Tax

Before enactment of a temporary provision in the American Recovery and Reinvestment Act of 2009, (ARRA; P.L. 111-5), the alternative minimum tax (AMT) treated the interest income from qualified private activity bonds differently than the interest income from governmental bonds.[18] The AMT is an income tax that is levied in parallel with the income tax and is intended to ensure that taxpayers with many deductions and exemptions pay a minimum percentage of their gross income in taxes.

Before ARRA, the interest income from tax-exempt private activity bonds was included in the alternative minimum tax (AMT) base and thus taxable. The temporary provision suspending the AMT taxability expires on January 1, 2011. Because private activity bonds will be included in the AMT after this date, the bonds carry a higher interest rate (approximately 50 basis points[19]) than do tax-exempt government-purpose bonds, all else equal.[20] However, the private activity bond rate is still lower than the taxable bond rate.

Repealing the AMT or exempting some bonds issued for qualified private activities from the AMT would increase investor demand for those bonds. The increased attractiveness of those bonds would eventually lead to lower interest costs for the issuer of qualified private activity bonds.

What is a Private Activity Bond?

A private activity bond is one that primarily benefits or is used by a private entity. The tax code defines *private business (or private entity) use* as " ... use (directly or indirectly) in a trade or business carried on by any person other than a governmental unit. For purposes of the preceding sentence, use as a member of the general public shall not be taken into account."[21] Two conditions or tests are used to assess the status of a bond issue with regard to the private entity test. Satisfying both conditions would mean the bonds are taxable private activity bonds. Bonds are *private activity bonds* and **not** tax-exempt if both of the following conditions are met:[22]

- [use test] more than 10% of the proceeds of the issue are to be used for any *private business use*,... [and]
- [security test] if the payment on the principal of, or the interest on, more than 10% of the proceeds of such issue is (under the terms of such issue or any underlying arrangement) directly or indirectly secured by any interest in (1) property used or to be used for a private business use, or (2) payments in respect to such property. Or [if the payment is] to be derived from payments (whether or not to the issuer) in respect of property, or borrowed money, used or to be used for a private business use.

If a bond issue passes both tests, the bonds are taxable and would carry a higher interest rate. Nevertheless, bond issues that pass both tests can still qualify for tax-exempt financing if they are identified in the tax code as *qualified* private activities. Thus, when those in the bond community refer to tax-exempt private activity bonds, the more technically correct reference is tax-exempt, *qualified* private activity bonds.

There is also a private loan financing test. Under this test, a bond is *not* tax-exempt if more than the lesser of 5% or $5 million of the proceeds of the issue is to be used directly or indirectly to make or finance loans to persons other than governmental persons.[23] For example, an issuer could not use the proceeds from a tax-exempt bond to loan money to small businesses for capital improvements.[24]

What Are the Qualified Private Activities?

A number of qualified private activities are granted special status in the tax code (see Table 2). These activities are called "qualified private activities" because they qualify for tax-exempt financing even though they would likely "pass" the two part private activity test or the private loan test which would otherwise disallow tax-exempt financing. The list of qualified private activities has gradually expanded to 22 activities from the 12 that were originally defined by the Revenue and Expenditure Control Act of 1968. The Tax Reform Act of 1986 kept most of the activities listed in the 1968 Act and reorganized the private activity bond section of the federal tax code.

The Revenue and Expenditure Control Act of 1968

The 1968 Act legislated that the interest payments on industrial development bonds (IDBs, the original private activity bonds) were to be included in taxable income. This was a shift from the previous Internal Revenue Service (IRS) position, which held that the interest on these bonds was not taxable income. The motivation behind the change offered in the 1968 Act was based " ... on the theory that industrial development bonds described in the proposed [IRS] regulations were not 'obligations of a State or any political subdivision' within the meaning of section 103 since the primary obligor was a not a State or political subdivision."[25] The 1968 Act also (1) established the basis for the current private use and private security tests; (2) created exceptions to the taxability provision for small issuers; (3) and specified a group of private activities that would qualify for tax-exempt bond financing.

The Tax Reform Act of 1986

The 1986 Act, which rewrote the Internal Revenue Code of 1954, renewed most of the previously defined private activities identified in the 1968 Act. Notably, TRA 1986 added one private activity, qualified hazardous waste facilities, and limited the exemption for some previously acceptable private activities, including construction of sports facilities and privately owned (as opposed to government owned) airports, docks, wharves, and mass-commuting facilities. In **Table 2**, the activities that must be government owned to qualify for tax-exempt financing are identified in italics. After enactment of TRA 1986, there were several other additions to the list of qualified private activities. The date of introduction for each qualified private activity is included in the last column of **Table 2**.

Empowerment Zones and New York Liberty Zones

In addition to private activities listed in **Table 2**, there are special zones where tax-exempt private activity bonds can be issued for qualified economic development projects in that zone. The Empowerment Zone / Enterprise Community (EZ) program has been implemented in rounds and each round is subject to different debt rules. Round I EZ bonds are subject to the state volume cap and each zone can have only $3 million of EZ bonds outstanding.[26] There are also limits on the amount of Round I EZ bonds any one borrower can have outstanding. An EZ borrower can have an aggregate of $20 million outstanding for all EZ projects throughout the country.

Round II EZs (and all EZs established after December 31, 2001) are subject to designation "lifetime" caps depending on the urban vs. rural designation and population for urban EZs. For the lifetime of the EZ designation, rural EZs can issue up to $60 million; urban EZs with population less than 100,000 can issue up to $130 million; and urban EZs with population greater than 100,000 can issue up to $230 million. In contrast to Round I EZs, there are no limits on the amount any one entity can borrow for Round II EZs.[27]

The New York Liberty Zone (NYLZ) was established in the wake of the September 11, 2001 terrorist attacks upon New York City.[28] The tax benefits created to foster economic revitalization within the NYLZ included a "Liberty Bond" program. The program allows New York State (in conjunction and coordination with New York City) to issue up to $8 billion of tax-exempt, private activity bonds for qualified facilities in the NYLZ. Qualified facilities follow the exempt facility rules within section 142 of the IRC. The original deadline to issue the bonds was January 1, 2005, but was extended to January 1, 2010, by P.L. 108-311.

The Safe, Accountable, Flexible, Efficient, Transportation Equity Act of 2005

This legislation created a new type of tax-exempt private activity bond for the construction of rail to highway (or highway to rail) transfer facilities. The national limit is $15 billion and the bonds are not subject to state volume caps for private activity bonds. The Secretary of Transportation allocates the bond authority on a project-by-project basis.

Gulf Opportunity Zone Act of 2005

The hurricanes that struck the gulf region in late summer 2005 prompted Congress to create a tax-advantaged economic development zone intended to encourage investment and rebuilding in the gulf region. The Gulf Opportunity Zone (GOZ) is comprised of the counties where the Federal Emergency Management Agency (FEMA) declared the inhabitants to be eligible for individual and public assistance. Based on proportion of state personal income, the Katrina-affected portion of the GOZ represents approximately 73% of Louisiana's economy, 69% of Mississippi's, and 18% of Alabama's.[29]

Specifically, the Gulf Opportunity Zone Act of 2005 (GOZA 2005; P.L. 109-35) contains two provisions that expanded the amount of private activity bonds outstanding and language to relax the eligibility rules for mortgage revenue bonds. The most significant is the provision to increase the volume cap (see **Table 3**) for private activity bonds issued for Hurricane Katrina recovery in Alabama, Louisiana, and Mississippi (identified as the Gulf Opportunity Zone, or "GO Zone"). GOZA 2005 added $2,500 per person in the federally declared Katrina disaster areas in which the residents qualify for individual and public assistance. The increased volume capacity added approximately $2.2 billion for Alabama, $7.8 billion for Louisiana, and $4.8 billion for Mississippi in aggregate over the next five years through 2010. The legislation defines "qualified project costs" that can be financed with the bond proceeds as (1) the cost of any qualified residential rental project (26 sec. 142(d)) and (2) the cost of acquisition, construction, reconstruction, and renovation of (i) non residential real property (including fixed improvements associated with such property) and (ii) public utility property (26 sec. 168(i)(10)) in the GOZ. The additional capacity has to be issued before January 1, 2011. The provision was estimated to cost $1.556 billion over the 2006-2015 budget window.[30]

The second provision allows for advance refunding of certain tax-exempt bonds. Under GOZA 2005, governmental bonds issued by Alabama, Louisiana, and Mississippi may be advance refunded an additional time and exempt facility private activity bonds for airports, docks, and wharves once. Private activity bonds are otherwise not eligible for advance refunding. Following is a brief description of advance refunding and how the GOZA 2005 provision confers a significant tax benefit to the gulf states.

Refunding is the practice of issuing new bonds to buy back outstanding bonds to potentially lower interest costs. *Advance* refunding is the practice of allowing the new bonds to be outstanding for longer than 90 days. Advance refunding, thus, allows for the existence of two sets of federally tax-exempt bond issues to be outstanding at the same time for a single project. GOZA 2005 allows the states of Alabama, Louisiana, and Mississippi to advance refund \$1.125 billion, \$4.5 billion, and \$2.25 billion, respectively. This provision was estimated to cost \$741 million over the 2006-2015 budget window.[31] For more on advance refunding, see CRS Report RL30638, *Tax-Exempt Bonds: A Description of State and Local Government Debt*, by Steven Maguire.

The Housing and Economic Recovery Act of 2008

In response to the housing crisis of 2008, Congress included two provisions in the Housing and Economic Recovery Act of 2008 (HERA; P.L. 110-289) that are intended to assist the housing sector. First, HERA provided that interest on qualified private activity bonds issued for (1) qualified residential rental projects, (2) qualified mortgage bonds, and (3) qualified veterans' mortgage bonds, would not be subject to the AMT. In addition, HERA also created an additional \$11 billion of volume cap space for bonds issued for qualified mortgage bonds and qualified bonds for residential rental projects. The cap space was designated for 2008 but can be carried forward through 2010.

The American Recovery and Reinvestment Act of 2009

In response to the financial crisis and economic recession, Congress included several bond-related provisions in the American Recovery and Reinvestment Act of 2009 (ARRA; P.L. 111-5). The following three provisions are intended to make bond finance less expensive for the designated facilities. One expanded the definition of qualified manufacturing facilities (under Sec. 144(a)(12)(C)) to include the creation and production of intangible property including patents, copyrights, formulae, etc. Before ARRA, only tangible property was eligible. The second created a new category of private activity bond called "recovery zone facility bonds." The bonds are to be used for investment in infrastructure, job training, education, and economic development in economically distressed areas. The bonds, which are subject to a separate national cap of $15 billion allocated to the states based on the decline in employment in 2008, are to be issued in 2009 and 2010.

A third provision provided $2 billion for tribal governments to issue tax-exempt for economic development purposes. The tax code currently allows tribal governments to issue debt for "essential government services" only. Many economic development projects would not qualify absent this ARRA provision.

IRS Review of Tax-Exempt Status

The IRS often reviews the tax-exempt status of outstanding bonds issued for *qualified* private activities. If the bonds that were originally issued as tax-exempt are found to no longer qualify (meaning that they pass both the security and use tests) the interest on the bonds becomes taxable. Technically, bond holders are the recipient of the tax benefit and are responsible for remitting forgone taxes to the Treasury when a tax-exempt bond fails to qualify. A *retroactive* taxability finding means all previous tax benefits to the bond holder would have to be returned to the Treasury. A *prospective* taxability finding means all future interest payments would be taxable to the bond holder. However, in most cases, the IRS will settle the apparent violation by requiring that the issuer, not the bond holders, pay a monetary penalty and that the issuer change the circumstances that led to the non-compliance finding.[32]

What Is the Private Activity Volume Cap?[33]

The federal government has limited the amount of private activity bonds that states can issue to a subset of the 22 activities listed in **Table 2** and to EZ bonds. The third column of **Table 2** identifies the 13 activities (of the 22) that are subject to an annual state volume cap. The annual cap was increased from the greater of $50 per capita or $150 million in 2000, to the greater of $90 per capita or $273.775 million in 2010 (and is adjusted annually for inflation). For small states, the $273.775 million minimum provides a more generous volume cap than the per capita allocation. **Table 3** lists the volume cap amount in 2009 and 2010 for all states and territories and compares the 2009 cap to state personal income in 2009.

Of the 13 activities subject to an annual volume cap, two are treated differently than the others, and four others are subject to a separate cap. First, states are required to count only 25% of the bonds issued for high-speed intercity rail facilities (26 U.S.C. 142(I)) against the annual cap. If the facility is government owned and operated, no cap allocation is required. Second, bonds issued for solid waste disposal facilities (26 U.S.C. 142(a)(6)) are not subject to the cap if the facility is government owned and operated.

Table 2. Qualified Private Activities

Internal Revenue Code Section	Type of Private Activity (Italicized activities must be owned by the issuing government to qualify)	Subject to Volume Cap	Year Established
Sec. 142	**Exempt facility bonds**		
Sec. 142(c)	Airports	No	1968
Sec. 142(c)	Docks and wharves	No	1968
Sec. 142(c)	Mass commuting facilities	Yes	1981
Sec. 142(e)	Water furnishing facilities	Yes	1968
Sec. 142(a)(5)	Sewage facilities	Yes	1968
Sec. 142(a)(6)	Solid waste disposal facilities	Yes/No[a]	1968
Sec. 142(d)	Qualified residential rental projects	Yes[b]	1968
Sec. 142(f)	Local electric energy or gas furnishing facility	Yes	1968
Sec. 142(g)	Local district heating and cooling facilities	Yes	1982
Sec. 142(h)	Qualified hazardous waste facilities	Yes	1986
Sec. 142(I)	High-speed intercity rail facilities	Yes[c]	1988
Sec. 142(j)	Environmental enhancements of hydroelectric generating facilities	No	1992

Internal Revenue Code Section	Type of Private Activity (Italicized activities must be owned by the issuing government to qualify)	Subject to Volume Cap	Year Established
Sec. 142(k)	Qualified public educational facilities	No[d]	2001
Sec. 142(l)	Qualified green building and sustainable design projects	No[d]	2005
Sec. 142(m)	Qualified highway and surface freight transfer facilities	No[d]	2005
Sec. 1400U-3	Recovery zone facility bonds	No[d]	2009
Sec. 143	**Mortgage revenue bonds**		
Sec. 143(a)	Qualified mortgage bond	Yes[b]	1968
Sec. 143(b)	Qualified veterans' mortgage bond	No	1968
Sec. 144(a)	**Qualified small issue bond**	Yes	1968
Sec. 144(b)	**Qualified student loan bond**	Yes	1976
Sec. 144(c)	**Qualified redevelopment bond**	Yes	1968
Sec. 145	**Qualified 501(c)(3) bond**	No	1968

a. Exempt from the cap if governmentally owned. Subject to the cap if privately owned.

b. Bonds for residential rental projects and mortgages were allocated an additional $11 billion for 2008 that can be carried forward through 2010 by the Housing Assistance Tax Act of 2008.

c. 25% of the bond issue is included in the cap. If the facility is owned by a governmental unit, no cap allocation is required. In addition, if the facility is not governmentally owned, to qualify for tax-exempt status, the owner must elect not to claim any depreciation deductions or investment tax credits with respect to the property financed with the bonds.

d. Educational facility bonds are subject to a separate state cap: the greater of $10 per capita or $5 million. Green building bonds are subject to a national aggregate amount of $2 billion through the expiration of the program, scheduled for October 1, 2009. Highway bonds are subject to the following annual issuance limits: $130 million in 2005; $750 million each year for 2006 through 2009; $1.87 billion in 2010; and $2 billion each year for 2011 through 2015, zero thereafter. Recovery zone facility bonds are subject to a separate cap of $15 billion.

Qualified public educational facilities (26 U.S.C. 142(k)) are subject to a separate annual cap which is the greater of $10 per capita or $5 million. The three activities, bonds for green buildings (26 U.S.C. 142(l)), highway-freight transfer facilities (26 U.S.C. 142(m)), and recovery zone facilities (26 U.S.C. 1400U-3) are subject to a separate cap. Green buildings are subject to a $2 billion lifetime (not annual) cap and transfer facilities are subject to annual national caps ranging from $130 million for 2005 rising to $2 billion from 2011 through 2015 (for a total of $15 billion).[34] The $15 billion of recovery zone facility bonds are allocated to the states by formula then are further sub-allocated to local jurisdictions, also by formula. Generally, a jurisdiction receives an allocation that matches its ratio of the total decrease in employment relative to the national decline in employment in 2008.[35]

The total 2010 private activity bond volume cap for all states and the District of Columbia is over $30 billion. California is allowed to issue over one-tenth of total new volume in 2010 or $3.3 billion (see **Table 3**). However, as measured against total California personal income, the new volume cap is considerably less than the national average. For every $100 of 2009 personal income in California, approximately $0.21 of private activity debt can be issued in 2010 whereas the U.S. average is $0.39.[36] In contrast, Vermont could issue up to $1.14 of private activity debt for every $100 of personal income (see the last column of **Table 3**). The less populous states are more likely to not use the entire annual cap amount for this reason.[37]

Table 3. Annual State Private Activity Bond Volume Cap, 2009 and 2010

State	2009 Volume Cap ($ millions)	2010 Volume Cap ($ millions)	2009 Personal Income ($ millions)	2010 Cap per $100 of 2009 Personal Income
Alabama	419.6	423.8	155,840	0.27
Alaska	273.3	273.8	29,757	0.92
Arizona	585.0	593.6	217,235	0.27
Arkansas	273.3	273.8	92,307	0.30
California	3,308.1	3,326.6	1,564,389	0.21
Colorado	444.6	452.2	207,742	0.22
Connecticut	315.1	316.6	191,385	0.17
Delaware	273.3	273.8	35,243	0.78
District of Columbia	273.3	273.8	39,578	0.69
Florida	1,649.6	1,668.4	700,361	0.24
Georgia	871.7	884.6	332,091	0.27

State	2009 Volume Cap ($ millions)	2010 Volume Cap ($ millions)	2009 Personal Income ($ millions)	2010 Cap per $100 of 2009 Personal Income
Hawaii	273.3	273.8	54,409	0.50
Idaho	273.3	273.8	48,898	0.56
Illinois	1,161.1	1,161.9	534,638	0.22
Indiana	573.9	578.1	216,618	0.27
Iowa	273.3	273.8	110,541	0.25
Kansas	273.3	273.8	106,875	0.26
Kentucky	384.2	388.3	137,546	0.28
Louisiana	397.0	404.3	159,499	0.25
Maine	273.3	273.8	48,441	0.57
Maryland	507.0	513.0	275,201	0.19
Massachusetts	584.8	593.4	328,858	0.18
Michigan	900.3	897.3	339,219	0.26
Minnesota	469.8	474.0	218,823	0.22
Mississippi	273.3	273.8	88,864	0.31
Missouri	532.0	538.9	213,610	0.25
Montana	273.3	273.8	33,154	0.83
Nebraska	273.3	273.8	68,417	0.40
Nevada	273.3	273.8	101,966	0.27
New Hampshire	273.3	273.8	56,732	0.48
New Jersey	781.4	783.7	438,111	0.18
New Mexico	273.3	273.8	66,304	0.41
New York	1,754.1	1,758.7	917,610	0.19
North Carolina	830.0	844.3	323,204	0.26
North Dakota	273.3	273.8	25,570	1.07
Ohio	1,033.7	1,038.8	408,395	0.25
Oklahoma	327.8	331.8	130,037	0.26
Oregon	341.1	344.3	136,449	0.25
Pennsylvania	1,120.3	1,134.4	498,868	0.23
Rhode Island	273.3	273.8	43,185	0.63
South Carolina	403.2	410.5	145,041	0.28
South Dakota	273.3	273.8	30,006	0.91
Tennessee	559.3	566.7	214,633	0.26
Texas	2,189.4	2,230.4	904,166	0.25

Table 3. (Continued)

State	2009 Volume Cap ($ millions)	2010 Volume Cap ($ millions)	2009 Personal Income ($ millions)	2010 Cap per $100 of 2009 Personal Income
Utah	273.3	273.8	85,975	0.32
Vermont	273.3	273.8	23,939	1.14
Virginia	699.2	709.4	345,841	0.21
Washington	589.4	599.8	278,236	0.22
West Virginia	273.3	273.8	58,631	0.47
Wisconsin	506.5	508.9	208,220	0.24
Wyoming	273.3	273.8	24,876	1.10
U.S. Total	30,251.5	30,856.9	12,015,535	0.39

Sources: Personal income data are from the Bureau of Census, State Annual Personal Income, available at http://www.bea.gov/bea/regional/spi/. Bond volume cap information for 2009 and 2010 is from the *Bond Buyer, SourceMedia Inc.*, 2010.

This disparity arises from the two part volume capacity calculation which provides for a minimum of $273.775 million, regardless of state population. In addition, states that have total personal income below the national average would also have a relatively high debt allowance as measured against personal income. The last column of **Table 3** provides a comparative measure of the state-by-state volume capacity based on 2009 personal income.

Allocation by Type of Activity

Each state independently determines the allocation of its volume capacity. Table 4 identifies the total cap distribution for private activities from 2004 through 2009. The category names were used by the *Bond Buyer* newspaper and were continued by the Council of Development Finance Agencies (CDFA). The CDFA assumed control of the survey from the *Bond Buyer* beginning in 2008.[38] The names used by the *Bond Buyer*/CDFA differ from the more detailed names for the private activities used in the tax code and listed in **Table 2**. Nevertheless, the data roughly reflect the cap allocation preferences of the states and their subdivisions. Note that roughly half of the available volume capacity in any given year is carried forward to the following year. In 2008 and 2009, HERA included an additional $11 billion in volume capacity for housing that is not included in the table.

Table 4. State Use of Volume Capacity, 2004 to 2009.

Bond Allocation	2004	2005	2006	2007	2008	2009
Total Volume Capacity Available	$43,088	$49,142	$48,675	$49,355	$45,802	$53,603
New Volume Capacity	25,741	26,079	26,438	28,185	28,571	30,252
Carryover from previous years	*17,347*	*23,063*	*23,277*	*21,170*	*17,231*	*23,351*
Carry forward to next year	22,950	26,337	22,638	16,523	24,262	34,367
Single-family Mortgage Revenue	5,204	6,507	10,093	9,546	3,705	3,571
Abandon Capacity	839	910	1,417	1,001	3,620	2,318
Exempt Facilities	1,646	1,915	2,605	2,612	2,578	2,352
Housing not Classified	186	822	562	1,983	2,489	930
Student Loans	4,723	5,124	4,018	4,423	1,548	1,369
Multi-family Housing	5,007	5,562	6,252	5,743	1,286	1,154
Industrial Development	797	1,000	1,195	3,081	1,266	947

Source: "State Allocations and Use of Private Activity Bonds in 2004," *The Bond Buyer*, May 2, 2005; "State Allocations and Use of Private Activity Bonds in 2005," *The Bond Buyer*, May 1, 2006; "State Allocations of Private Activity Bonds in 2006," *The Bond Buyer*, June 27, 2007; and "State Allocations of Private Activity Bonds in 2007," *The Bond Buyer*, June 10, 2008. Data for 2008 and 2009 are from the Council on Development Finance Agencies, "CDFA's 2008 National Volume Cap Report," released July 2009 and "CDFA's 2008 National Volume Cap Report," released August 2010.

Notes: The totals may not sum precisely because of rounding and small survey changes from year to year. In addition, some states may report totals with specifying purpose.

The amount of capacity dedicated to mortgage revenue bonds (MRBs) varies significantly over the five years examined, though was always the most common use of the volume cap. For example, in 2006, $10.1 billion was used for MRBs and in 2009 the amount had dropped to $3.6 billion. Note that in 2008, of the additional allocation of $11 billion for MRBs included in the HERA of 2008, just over $2 billion was allocated in 2008 with the remainder carried forward. As noted earlier, the new capacity under HERA can be carried forward through 2010.

Unused volume capacity can be carried forward for up to three years, as long as the state identifies the project for which the cap space is dedicated. Bond capacity that has not been used after three years is then abandoned. Abandoned bond capacity rose considerably in 2008.

Other Restrictions on Private Activity Bonds

The use of private activity bonds is also limited by other technical restrictions. In general, loosening the restrictions would allow issuers to reduce administrative and compliance costs. However, the relaxed restrictions would exacerbate the concerns (i.e., the economically inefficient allocation of capital) surrounding tax-exempt bonds that were discussed earlier in the report. Following is a list of the more technical rules along with the section in the tax code where the rule appears.

- The maturity of the bonds cannot be greater than 120% of the economic life of the asset purchased with the bonds (26 U.S.C. 147(b));
- less than 25% of the bond proceeds can be used to acquire land (except for qualified first-time farmers) (26 U.S.C. 147(c));
- proceeds of the bond issue cannot be used to purchase existing property unless greater than 15% of the cost of acquiring the property is spent on rehabilitating the property (26 U.S.C. 147(d));
- public approval of bonds, either through public hearing and notice or voter referendum, is required for private activity bonds (26 U.S.C. 147(f)); and
- issuance costs cannot be any greater than 2% of the bond proceeds (3.5% for mortgage bond issues of less than $20 million) (26 U.S.C. 147(g)).
- private activity bonds cannot be advance refunded.[39]

CONCLUSION AND FURTHER READING

The history, tax laws, financial properties, and economic effects of tax-exempt bonds are all exceedingly complex and continually evolving. This report is intended to clarify part of the tax- exempt bond labyrinth. Nevertheless, the reader may wish to explore tax-exempt bonds in more depth or from a more general, less technical perspective. The following reading list should equip the reader with a good foundation for pursuit of either objective.

Bruce Davie and Dennis Zimmerman, "Tax-Exempt Bonds After the South Carolina Decision," *Tax Notes*, vol. 39, no. 13, June 27, 1988, p. 1573.

Peter Fortune, "Tax-Exempt Bonds Really Do Subsidize Municipal Capital!," *National Tax Journal*, vol. 51, no. 1, March 1998, p. 43.

Roger H. Gordon and Gilbert E. Metcalf, "Do Tax-Exempt Bonds Really Subsidize Municipal Capital?," *National Tax Journal*, vol. 44, no. 4, part 1, December 1991, p. 71.

Walter Hellerstein and Eugene W. Haper, "Discriminatory State Taxation of Private Activity Bonds After *Davis*," *State Tax Notes*, April 27, 2009, p. 295.

George J. Marlin and Joe Mysak, *The Guidebook to Municipal Bonds: The History, The Industry, The Mechanics* (New York: The American Banker/Bond Buyer, 1991).

David J. Ott and Allan H. Meltzer, *Federal Tax Treatment of State and Local Securities* (Washington, D.C.: The Brookings Institution, 1963).

Judy Wesalo Temel, *The Fundamentals of Municipal Bonds, 5th Edition* (New York: John Wiley and Sons, 2001).

Dennis Zimmerman, *The Private Use of Tax-Exempt Bonds: Controlling Public Subsidy of Private Activity* (Washington, D.C.: The Urban Institute Press, 1991).

End Notes

[1] The tax-exemption is provided for in 26 U.S.C. 103.

[2] The Internal Revenue Service (IRS) uses a two part test to classify an activity as a private activity. This test will be explained in more detail later in the report. Generally, activities are classified as "private" because private individuals and businesses benefit directly from debt issued by the state or local government.

[3] 26 U.S.C. 141 describes requirements for qualified private activity bonds.

[4] Before this act was passed, state and local government usually issued bearer bonds that paid principal and interest to whomever presented the bond to the issuer (or the issuer's agent,

usually a bank). In contrast, a registered bond includes the owner's name on the bond and a change in ownership must be registered with the issuer (or the issuer's agent). For a full discussion of the impact of the South Carolina vs. Baker case on tax-exempt bonds, see Bruce Davie and Dennis Zimmerman, "Tax-Exempt Bonds After the South Carolina Decision," *Tax Notes*, vol. 39, no. 13, June 27, 1988, p. 1573.

[5] *State of South Carolina vs. J.A. Baker, Secretary of the Treasury*: Supreme Court of the United States, April 20, 1988. 485 U.S. 505.

[6] Ibid.

[7] U.S. Congress, Joint Committee on Taxation, General Explanation of the Revenue Provisions of the Deficit Reduction Act of 1984, 98th Cong., 2nd sess. (Washington: GPO, 1984), p. 930.

[8] U.S. Congress, Joint Committee on Taxation, General Explanation of the Tax Reform Act of 1986, 100th Cong., 1st sess. (Washington: GPO, 1987), p. 1151.

[9] For a comprehensive economic assessment of private activity bonds, see Dennis Zimmerman, *The Private Use of Tax-Exempt Bonds: Controlling Public Subsidy of Private Activity* (Washington, D.C.: The Urban Institute Press, 1991).

[10] The discussion here does not address the effect of state taxes on the tax-exempt debt of other states. For example, taxpayers in Virginia must pay Virginia income taxes on the tax-exempt (exempt from federal income taxes) debt of other states. However, Virginia taxpayers do not have to pay income taxes on interest earned on Virginia bonds.

[11] The calculation is: 7.00% multiplied by (0.65=1 .00-.35) equals 4.55%.

[12] Clearly, there are significant differences between corporate bonds and bonds issued by a governmental entity extending beyond the tax status. For example, a typical tax-exempt bond will include a call provision allowing the issuer to recall the bond after a fixed period (often 10 years). In addition, disclosure requirements for municipal issuers are usually less transparent than for public corporations.

[13] Market participants also use the comparison between the interest rate on tax-exempt bonds and 10-year Treasury bonds.

[14] For example, someone in the 10% income tax bracket would find tax-exempt bonds attractive only if the interest rate were 6.3 7%. Or, looking at the problem from a different perspective, the marginal tax rate below which tax-exempt bonds are not attractive is 16.58%. Thus, taxpayers in marginal tax brackets below this rate would not find tax-exempt bonds attractive investments because the market interest rate on municipal bonds would be too low. Taxpayers in the 15% marginal tax bracket would receive a higher after-tax return though buying taxable bonds and paying taxes on the interest income at the 15% rate.

[15] A persistent anomaly exists for long-term, tax-exempt municipal bonds. The interest-rate spread between tax-exempt bonds and taxable bonds is smaller for long-term bonds (the long end of the so-called yield curve) than for short-term bonds. Thus, the implicit tax rate for long–term municipal bonds is smaller than for shorter term bonds. One explanation is that the tax treatment of tax-exempt bonds and taxable bonds is not symmetrical through the yield curve. The lower tax rate for capital gain income plays a role in this phenomena. For more, see Green, Richard C., "A Simple Model of the Taxable and Tax-Exempt Yield Curves," *The Review of Financial Studies*, vol. 6, no. 2, summer 1993, pp. 233-264.

[16] Interest rate averages are composites of a variety of bond issues and provide a good benchmark for market interest rates for municipal bonds.

[17] For more, see CRS Report 98-856, *Federal Reserve Interest Rate Changes: 2001-2009*, by Marc Labonte.

[18] Interest income from qualified private activity bonds for 501(c)(3) projects and housing projects are excluded from the AMT.

[19] 50 basis points is equivalent to one-half of a percentage point or 0.50%.

[20] Jacob Fine, "AMT Spreads on the Rise," *The Bond Buyer*, July 26, 2000, p. 1.

[21] 26 U.S.C. 141(b)(6)(A)

[22] 26 U.S.C. 141(b)

[23] 26 U.S.C. 141(c).

[24] The tax code does allow some loan programs to be financed with tax-exempt bonds such as mortgage bonds. These special cases are described in more detail later in the report.

[25] U.S. Congress, Conference Committees, 1968, Revenue and Expenditure Control Act of 1968, conference report to accompany H.R. 15414, House Report No. 1533, 90th Cong., 2nd sess. (Washington: GPO, 1968), p. 32.

[26] A special EZ for the District of Columbia allows up to $15 million of outstanding EZ bond debt.

[27] See the following publication for more details on the EZ programs: U.S. Department of Housing and Urban Development, *Tax Incentive Guide for Businesses in the Renewal Communities, Empowerment Zones, and Enterprise Communities: FY2003.* The report is available at the Department of Housing and Urban Development website: http://www.hud.gov/offices/cpd/economicdevelopment/library/taxguide2003.pdf.

[28] Section 301 of the *Job Creation and Worker Assistance Act of 2002*, P.L. 107-147, created the various NYLZ tax benefits (26 U.S.C. 1400L). The tax-exempt bond component can be found in 26 U.S.C. 1400L(d).

[29] See CRS Report RL33 154, *The Impact of Hurricane Katrina on the State Budgets of Alabama, Louisiana, and Mississippi*, by Steven Maguire.

[30] The 10-year revenue loss estimates for GOZA 2005 are from the Joint Committee on Taxation, *Estimated Revenue Effects of H.R. 4440, the 'Gulf Opportunity Tax Relief Act of 2005,'* as passed by the House of Representatives and the Senate on Dec. 16, 2005, JCX-89-05, Dec. 20, 2005.

[31] JCT, Dec. 20, 2005.

[32] See the following IRS website for more information on tax-exempt bond rulings and findings: http://www.irs.gov/ compliance/index.html.

[33] 26 U.S.C. 146.

[34] For more on the transfer facility private activity bond program, see U.S. Department of Transportation, "Applications for Authority for Tax-Exempt Financing of Highway Projects and Rail-Truck Transfer Facilities," 71 *Federal Register* 642, Jan. 5, 2006.

[35] The IRS has established the following website to report those allocations: http://www.irs.gov/pub/irs-tege/rzblocalreallocations.pdf.

[36] The states were each given equal weight for the average calculation. The values in the last column of Table 3 were summed then divided by 51.

[37] For more on state use of the volume cap, see CRS Report RL34 159, *Private Activity Bonds: An Analysis of State Use, 2001 to 2006*, by Steven Maguire.

[38] The *Bond Buyer* administered the survey to collect the data for 2004 through 2006. In 2007, the Council of Development Finance Agencies began administering the survey and publishing the results.

[39] Current refunding is the practice of issuing bonds to replace existing bonds. Issuers typically do this to "lock-in" lower interest rates or more favorable borrowing terms. Current refunding is allowed as long as the "old" bonds are redeemed within 90 days of the issuance of the refunding bonds. Advance refunding is the practice of issuing new bonds to replace existing bonds, but not immediately (within 90 days) retiring the old bonds. Thus, two sets of tax-exempt bonds are outstanding for the same project.

In: Private Activity, Tax-Exempt and Tax Credit… ISBN: 978-1-61470-227-6
Editor: Fredrick Kjellson

Chapter 2

PRIVATE ACTIVITY BONDS: AN ANALYSIS OF STATE USE, 2001 TO 2006

Steven Maguire and Heather Durkin Negley

SUMMARY

State and local governments often issue debt instruments in exchange for the use of individuals' and businesses' savings. This debt obligates state and local governments to make interest payments for the use of these savings and to repay, at some time in the future, the amount borrowed. State and local governments finance capital facilities with debt rather than out of current tax revenue in order to match the time pattern of benefits from these capital facilities with the time pattern of tax payments.

The federal government subsidizes the cost of most state and local debt by excluding the interest income from federal income taxation. This tax exemption of interest income is granted because it is believed that state and local capital facilities will be under-provided if state and local taxpayers have to pay the full cost.

Generally, state and local governments issue two types of tax-exempt bonds: (1) governmental bonds and (2) private activity bonds. A portion of private activity bonds are subject to a federally legislated state-specific annual limit. The annual limit for each state is the greater of (1) state population from the previous year multiplied by an inflation adjusted dollar amount ($85 in 2008); or (2) an inflation adjusted annual minimum ($262.095 million in

2008). Most private activity bond volume (62.4%), however, is not subject to the state volume cap. This report identifies how each state, over the previous several years, has allocated private activity bond volume, including abandoned volume capacity.

The report also discusses the expansion of the types of projects eligible for private activity bond financing since 2001. Approximately $55 billion in new private activity bond volume has been created by Congress since 2001. A series of estimates by the Joint Committee on Taxation suggests that the new bonds would reduce federal tax revenue by as much as $5.6 billion. In the 110th Congress, various new proposals would further expand the types of private activities eligible for tax-exempt financing and modify the rules for existing qualified private activities. A selected group of legislative proposals are listed and summarized in this report including the proposed additional $10 billion in private activity bond capacity for housing.

OVERVIEW

Observers of the bond market group tax-exempt state and local government bonds into two broad categories: governmental and private activity.[1] Broadly speaking, Congress limits the use of tax-exempt private activity bonds (PABs) to selected activities. Recently, the opportunity to issue PABs has expanded as Congress has increased the range of projects and activities that qualify for tax-exempt status. This report focuses on state use of private activity bonds and the recently added activities eligible for tax-exempt financing. Approximately $55 billion of additional capacity has been added since 2001. In separate estimates, the Joint Committee on Taxation (JCT) projected that these new provisions would reduce federal tax revenue by approximately $5.6 billion over a 10-year period.[2]

In the 110th Congress, several legislative proposals have been introduced that would likely expand the volume of private activity bonds including housing stimulus legislation that would increase housing PAB volume by $10 billion (H.R. 5720 and H.R. 3221). The next section describes governmental and private activity bonds in more depth and is followed by a presentation of recently published bond data. The last section discusses legislation.

Table 1. New Money, Private Activity Bond Volume, by Activity and State, 2005 ("d" Indicates IRS Deleted the Data to Avoid Possible Disclosure of Taxpayer Information)

State	Total Amount Issued (in millions)	Percent of Total Amount Issued in 2005							
		Airports, Docks, and Wharves	Water, Sewage, & Solid Waste Disposal	Residential Rental	Mortgage	Small Issue	Hospital	501(c)(3) Nonhospital	All Other Bondsa
US Total	$54,691	6.0%	3.4%	11.8%	12.1%	1.3%	22.4%	28.8%	14.3%
Alabama	$244	0.0%	0.0%	d	0.0%	d	45.1%	46.3%	0.0%
Alaska	$229	0.0%	0.0%	d	0.0%	0.0%	0.0%	d	d
Arizona	$1,562	0.0%	10.9%	d	7.2%	0.0%	68.1%	2.6%	d
Arkansas	$292	0.0%	d	0.0%	0.0%	0.0%	d	14.7%	d
California	$4,804	1.8%	5.1%	30.0%	2.0%	0.5%	23.1%	30.7%	6.7%
Colorado	$1,319	0.0%	0.0%	9.1%	6.6%	d	27.5%	45.3%	d
Connecticut	$776	0.0%	d	d	27.6%	0.0%	0.0%	66.1%	d
Delaware	$189	0.0%	0.0%	d	d	0.0%	39.7%	d	d
District of Columbia	$1,000	d	0.0%	16.3%	0.0%	0.0%	d	20.8%	d
Florida	$2,004	10.3%	d	12.3%	5.8%	2.7%	21.5%	42.6%	d
Georgia	$1,757	d	d	9.4%	d	2.8%	39.6%	44.5%	d
Hawaii	d	d	d	d	d	d	d	d	d
Idaho	$259	0.0%	d	0.0%	57.9%	d	d	4.2%	0.0%

Table 1. (Continued)

State	Total Amount Issued (in millions)	Percent of Total Amount Issued in 2005							
		Airports, Docks, and Wharves	Water, Sewage, & Solid Waste Disposal	Residential Rental	Mortgage	Small Issue	Hospital	501(c)(3) Nonhospital	All Other Bondsa
Illinois	$1,960	d	d	13.3%	11.8%	2.6%	21.9%	47.6%	0.0%
Indiana	$1,668	d	11.8%	d	d	2.2%	55.1%	13.6%	d
Iowa	$510	0.0%	d	d	28.8%	4.7%	28.4%	20.4%	15.9%
Kansas	$185	0.0%	d	d	57.8%	9.2%	d	15.7%	0.0%
Kentucky	$538	d	7.2%	9.5%	25.7%	d	18.0%	16.4%	d
Louisiana	$596	d	d	d	28.7%	0.0%	34.9%	2.2%	d
Maine	$300	d	d	12.7%	38.0%	d	0.0%	27.0%	d
Maryland	$914	0.0%	0.0%	14.3%	14.3%	d	d	67.0%	0.0%
Massachusetts	$1,782	d	0.0%	6.4%	d	1.5%	33.1%	43.2%	d
Michigan	$2,320	d	d	5.1%	0.0%	1.2%	37.3%	8.8%	23.6%
Minnesota	$1,258	d	d	9.3%	14.7%	1.4%	17.4%	44.9%	6.0%
Mississippi	$217	d	0.0%	d	d	8.8%	d	d	d
Missouri	$1,320	d	d	16.4%	12.1%	1.1%	34.6%	18.0%	d
Montana	$86	0.0%	0.0%	0.0%	d	0.0%	0.0%	d	0.0%
Nebraska	$248	0.0%	d	0.0%	d	0.8%	18.1%	43.5%	0.0%

State	Total Amount Issued (in millions)	Percent of Total Amount Issued in 2005							
		Airports, Docks, and Wharves	Water, Sewage, & Solid Waste Disposal	Residential Rental	Mortgage	Small Issue	Hospital	501(c)(3) Nonhospital	All Other Bondsa
Nevada	$359	0.0%	d	12.5%	0.0%	0.0%	39.3%	d	d
New Hampshire	$357	0.0%	21.8%	d	33.9%	0.0%	0.0%	17.1%	d
New Jersey	$1,274	0.0%	2.4%	9.8%	d	3.3%	20.1%	43.0%	d
New Mexico	$246	0.0%	0.0%	16.7%	d	d	d	0.0%	d
New York	$6,823	16.2%	0.9%	22.0%	4.0%	0.3%	5.1%	21.1%	30.4%
North Carolina	$1,611	d	d	d	d	1.0%	17.9%	23.5%	d
North Dakota	$244	0.0%	0.0%	0.0%	d	d	16.8%	11.1%	0.0%
Ohio	$1,518	d	5.3%	3.2%	d	1.6%	23.5%	34.0%	d
Oklahoma	$404	0.0%	0.0%	d	18.1%	0.2%	d	45.0%	d
Oregon	$333	0.0%	0.0%	24.0%	0.0%	d	d	46.5%	d
Pennsylvania	$2,937	d	5.7%	d	11.3%	2.6%	28.7%	43.4%	d
Rhode Island	$314	d	0.0%	d	d	d	d	53.8%	0.0%
South Carolina	$417	0.0%	d	9.4%	d	d	0.0%	15.3%	d
South Dakota	$456	0.0%	0.0%	0.0%	95.6%	1.1%	0.0%	3.3%	0.0%
Tennessee	$911	d	0.0%	8.1%	19.2%	d	d	36.8%	d

Table 1. (Continued)

State	Total Amount Issued (in millions)	Percent of Total Amount Issued in 2005							
		Airports, Docks, and Wharves	Water, Sewage, & Solid Waste Disposal	Residential Rental	Mortgage	Small Issue	Hospital	501(c)(3) Nonhospital	All Other Bondsa
Texas	$2,821	d	3.2%	18.5%	2.8%	d	20.9%	22.0%	31.0%
Utah	$543	0.0%	0.0%	d	23.0%	d	0.0%	51.2%	d
Vermont	$214	0.0%	0.0%	7.5%	d	0.0%	d	6.1%	d
Virginia	$1,821	6.5%	d	10.7%	d	0.5%	23.8%	16.1%	d
Washington	$1,199	d	3.8%	21.2%	d	1.2%	16.8%	37.1%	10.3%
West Virginia	$240	0.0%	0.0%	d	42.5%	d	45.8%	d	d
Wisconsin	$888	d	d	2.8%	38.4%	2.5%	26.1%	25.2%	0.0%
Wyoming	$378	0.0%	d	0.0%	37.8%	0.0%	0.0%	d	d

Source: CRS calculations based on data from: Cynthia Belmonte, "Tax-Exempt Bonds, 2005," *SOI Bulletin*, Fall 2007, vol. 27, no. 2.

a. The "all other bonds" category includes all issues for which a specific purpose either did not apply or was not clearly indicated on the Form 8038 return, as well as bonds for: local furnishing of energy or gas, local district heating or cooling facilities, hazardous waste facilities, facilities issued under a transitional rule of the TRA 1986, mass commuting facilities, qualified enterprise zone facility bonds, qualified empowerment zone facility bonds, District of Columbia Enterprise Zone facility bonds, Liberty bonds, veterans' mortgage bonds, student loan bonds, redevelopment bonds, and nongovernmental output property bonds.

Governmental Bonds

Governmental bonds are issued by state and local governments to finance governmental activities and public infrastructure construction such as roads, courthouses, and schools. The bonds are tax-exempt, meaning the holder does not have to pay income taxes on the interest income earned on the bonds. There is no federal limit on the volume of governmental bonds. In 2005, roughly 19,591 governmental bonds were issued, with a total volume of $311.3 billion.[3] This total includes "new money" and bonds used to refund outstanding debt. In 2005, 14,939 "new money" bonds were issued with a face value of $151 billion. Refunding bonds are typically issued during periods of relatively low interest rates.

Private Activity Bonds

In contrast to governmental bonds, Congress places restrictions on the issuance of private activity bonds (PABs) to limit their use. PABs are bonds where (1) more than 10% of the activity financed by the bonds is private activity and (2) more than 10% of the revenue used to repay the bonds is generated by activity at the financed facility. Congress has identified a subset of private activities that can be financed with tax-exempt bonds. The so-called *qualified* PABs, thus, are more like governmental bonds. Some qualified PABs are subject to a federally imposed annual state-by-state limit or "cap." Other qualified PABs are subject to a national limit, a separate state cap, or no cap at all.

The IRS reports that in 2005, total PAB "new money" volume was $54.7 billion and of that, $20.5 billion was subject to the volume cap. Each state is free to select the mix of qualified activities and to determine the total amount of private activity bond volume under the cap. Most states use the total annual volume cap, though some states do "abandon" capacity — that is, leave some capacity unused.

State use of PABs is of interest to Congress as the number of activities eligible for tax-exempt financing has expanded significantly since 1986 and accelerated since 2001.[4] If additional new activities are subject to the same cap as existing activities, competition for cap space could limit the effectiveness of the tax preferences for these activities. In addition, expanding the number of private activities eligible for tax-exempt financing, particularly proposals with separate caps, may influence the market for governmental bonds, as the new bonds would put upward pressure on market interest rates. Higher interest rates, in turn, may constrain the ability of some state and local governments to issue debt. And finally, issuing more tax-exempt bonds would reduce federal revenues, contributing to a larger budget deficit. Congressional action in the tax-exempt, private activity bond market will have a disparate impact on the states, as each state has different objectives for PABs.

The next section uses two data sources to analyze the activities financed by private activity bonds in each state. The first set of data, from the Internal Revenue Service (IRS), examines all state and local bonds issued in 2005. The second set of data, from a survey administered by the *Bond Buyer* publication, a unit of Thomson Financial Inc., is more narrowly focused on bonds subject to the volume cap and includes data for 2001 through 2006.

Use of Private Activity Bonds

Periodically, the Internal Revenue Service (IRS) compiles bond data contained in the information return, Form 8038.[5] This form is filed by issuers of tax-exempt bonds. In 2005, the most recent year where IRS data are available, *new money*, longterm *governmental* bonds raised a total of $151.6 billion, with $53.4 billion (35.3%) used for education. Bonds identified as "new money" are in contrast to "refunding" bonds. "New money" means the bond proceeds are to be used for a new project and are not used to retire outstanding debt. By comparison, also in 2005, state and local governments issued $54.7 billion of long-term, new money, *private activity* bonds (about 26.5% of new money, long-term tax-exempt debt). Most private activity bond volume is issued for non-profit organizations and hospitals ($27.969 billion).

Private Activity Bond Issuance by State

Not all PABs are subject to the federally imposed cap. Notably, the bonds issued for nonprofit activities are not subject to the volume cap (see **Table 1**). In fact, just over half of the amount of private activity bonds are subject to the state volume cap (55% of the $54.7 billion). After bonds issued for non-profit organizations, the next two largest categories are housing related bond issues. The variation among states, however, is significant. The variation is due in part to the timing of large projects and the preferences of citizens. For example, in Idaho, Montana, and Nebraska, over 50% of private activity bond volume was used for mortgage bonds, considerably higher than the average across all states of 10.5 8%.[6]

The IRS data in **Table 1**, though generally instructive, do not provide sufficiently detailed information on the amount and allocation of private activity bonds that are subject to the state-by-state volume cap to permit detailed analysis. More detail about the bonds subject to the cap would help federal policymakers analyze options for either expanding or reducing the private activities eligible for tax- exempt financing.

The Volume Cap on Private Activity Bonds

The current structure of the annual limit on PABs was first implemented as part of the Deficit Reduction Act of 1984 (P.L. 98-369). In that year, the statewide annual volume cap was the greater of $150 per capita or $200 million. In 1986, in addition to myriad other changes to the private activity bond rules and tax-exempt bonds more generally, the Tax Reform Act of 1986 (TRA 1986, P.L. 99-514) reduced the volume cap to the greater of $50 per capita or $150 million, effective in 1988. The volume cap remained unchanged until 1998 when the Omnibus Appropriations Act of 1998 (OBRA98, P.L. 105-277) increased the volume cap to the greater of $55 per capita or $165 million, beginning in 2003. The 1998 rules were superceded in 2000 by the Community Renewal Tax Relief Act of 2000 (CRTRA, P.L. 106-554), which indexed the per capita and minimum amounts for inflation.

Table 2 reports the per capita and minimum limits for 2001 through 2008 under current law. States choose the greater of the per capita amount multiplied by state population or the annual minimum amount. In most years, 21 less populous states and the District of Columbia are subject to the annual minimum.[7] If population grows significantly faster than the inflation index used to increase the cap, then the per capita amount is determinative.

The volume cap was originally introduced to limit the use of tax-exempt private activity bonds and to encourage states to prioritize projects, as volume cap space was intentionally scarce. Since 2001, however, Congress has enacted legislation creating new types of private activities not subject to the existing state-by-state cap. Congress has also allowed selected private activity bonds to "advance refund" existing debt under the same recently passed legislation.[8] The total new volume capacity of these new private activity bonds is at least $54.8 billion (see **Table 3**). The new volume authorized under the bond legislation enacted from 2001 to 2005 was $54.8 billion. This amount is in addition to the pre-existing total volume cap available for all states and the District of Columbia over the same time period of $146.0 billion (see **Table 5**).

Private Activity Bonds Subject to Volume Cap by State

Table 4 compares the IRS data to the *Bond Buyer* data for 2005 and also reports the 2006 *Bond Buyer* data. For each year, the *Bond Buyer* data is for bonds subject to the cap. The difference between the two amounts is likely attributable to two factors. First, the *Bond Buyer* data include the bond capacity carried forward from previous years, and second, the definitions used by the *Bond Buyer* are not the same as the IRS definitions. For more robust analysis, the IRS data would need to include more detail on the type of activity financed, by state, but for taxpayer confidentiality reasons, the IRS has not reported these data.[9] Thus, to assess more than the magnitude of private activity bond volume for each state, one must rely on data provided by the *Bond Buyer*.

Table 2. State Private Activity Bond Annual Volume Limits, 2001 to 2008

Year	States Choose the Greater of the Per Capita Amount Multiplied by Population or the Minimum	
	Per Capita Amount	State Annual Minimum Amount (in thousands)
2001	$62.50	$187,500
2002	$75.00	$225,000
2003	$75.00	$228,600
2004	$80.00	$233,795
2005	$80.00	$239,180
2006	$80.00	$246,610
2007	$85.00	$256,235
2008	$85.00	$262,095
Percentage Change 2001 to 2008	36.00%	39.78%
Total for 2001 to 2006 period		$1,360,685

Source: 26 U.S.C § 146(d).

Table 3. New Private Activity Bond Volume Created Since 2001

Facility Purpose	Year Authorized	Code Section	New Volume Authorized (in millions)	Estimated Revenue Loss (in millions)
Public Education[a]	2001	142(a)(13)	$15,000	$1,404
New York Liberty Zone[b]	2002	1400L	$8,000	$1,714
Green Building[c]	2004	142(a)(14)	$2,000	$231
Highway and Surface Transfer[d]	2005	142(a)(15)	$15,000	$738
Gulf Opport-unity Zone[e]	2005	1400N	$14,800	$1,556
Total			**$54,800**	**$5,643**

Sources: The revenue loss estimates are from: U.S. Congress, Joint Committee on Taxation, *General Explanation of Tax Legislation Enacted in the 107th Congress*, 107th Cong., 2nd sess. (Washington: GPO, 2003); U.S. Congress, Joint Committee on Taxation, *General Explanation of Tax Legislation Enacted in the 108th Congress*, 1 08th Cong., 1st sess. (Washington: GPO, 2005); U.S. Congress, Joint Committee on Taxation, *General Explanation of Tax Legislation Enacted in the 1 09th Congress*, 1 09th Cong., 2nd sess. (Washington: GPO, 2007).

a. Created by P.L. 107-16; the volume cap is $3 billion per year for five years (2001 to 2005) and the revenue loss is for the 2001-2012 budget window.

b. Created by P.L. 107-147 and modified by P.L. 108-311. The revenue loss represents the original cost (2001-2012 budget window) estimate plus the cost of the modification (2003-2014). The advance refunding provisions in the two bills increased the revenue cost $1.03 billion and is not included in the revenue loss reported in the table.

c. Created by P.L. 108-357.

d. Created by P.L. 109-59. The volume limit is to be split between highway projects and transfer facility projects. The revenue loss is for the 2005-2016 budget window.

e. Created by P.L. 109-135. The volume limit is estimated based on the population of the three states eligible for the bonds: Alabama ($2.2 billion); Louisiana ($7.8 billion); and Mississippi ($4.8 billion). The revenue loss is for the 2005-2016 budget window. The legislation includes an advance refunding provision that would cost $741 million and is not reflected in the table amount.

Table 4. Comparison of IRS and Bond Buyer Private Activity Bond Data, by State ("d" Indicates IRS Deleted the Data to Avoid Possible Disclosure of Taxpayer Information)

State	2005 IRS Data		Bond Buyer Data	
	Total Volume	Subject to Cap	2005 Cap Volume	2006 Cap Volume
US Total	**$54,691.0**	**$20,525.8**	**$26,079.1**	**$26,437.5**
Alabama	$244.0	$20.8	$362.4	$364.6
Alaska	$229.0	d	$239.2	$246.6
Arizona	$1,562.0	$458.8	$459.5	$475.1
Arkansas	$292.0	d	$239.2	$246.6
California	$4,804.0	$2,001.0	$2,871.5	$2,890.6
Colorado	$1,319.0	$357.4	$368.1	$373.2
Connecticut	$776.0	$262.3	$280.3	$280.8
Delaware	$189.0	$96.5	$239.2	$246.6
D.C.	$1,000.0	$162.8	$239.2	$246.1
Florida	$2,004.0	$443.6	$1,391.8	$1,423.2
Georgia	$1,757.0	$268.7	$706.4	$725.8
Hawaii	d	d	$239.2	$246.6
Idaho	$259.0	$162.0	$239.2	$246.6
Illinois	$1,960.0	$595.8	$1,012.3	$1,021.1
Indiana	$1,668.0	$377.6	$499.0	$501.8
Iowa	$510.0	$238.1	$239.2	$246.6
Kansas	$185.0	$149.6	$239.2	$246.6
Kentucky	$538.0	$338.7	$331.7	$333.9
Louisiana	$596.0	$355.4	$361.3	$361.9
Maine	$300.0	$216.2	$239.2	$246.6
Maryland	$914.0	$270.8	$444.6	$448.0
Massachusetts	$1,782.0	$393.4	$513.3	$511.9
Michigan	$2,320.0	$728.5	$809.0	$809.7
Minnesota	$1,258.0	$408.4	$408.1	$410.6
Mississippi	$217.0	$188.0	$239.2	$246.6
Missouri	$1,320.0	$594.5	$460.4	$464.0
Montana	$86.0	d	$239.2	$246.6
Nebraska	$248.0	$95.4	$239.2	$246.6
Nevada	$359.0	$174.5	$239.2	$246.6
New Hampshire	$357.0	$295.8	$239.2	$246.6

State	2005 IRS Data		Bond Buyer Data	
	Total Volume	Subject to Cap	2005 Cap Volume	2006 Cap Volume
New Jersey	$1,274.0	$469.9	$695.9	$697.4
New Mexico	$246.0	$218.2	$239.2	$246.6
New York	$6,823.0	$1,859.6	$1,538.2	$1,540.4
North Carolina	$1,611.0	$899.3	$683.3	$694.7
North Dakota	$244.0	$175.9	$239.2	$246.6
Ohio	$1,518.0	$636.6	$916.7	$917.1
Oklahoma	$404.0	$189.6	$281.9	$283.8
Oregon	$333.0	$83.1	$287.6	$291.3
Pennsylvania	$2,937.0	$651.0	$992.5	$994.4
Rhode Island	$314.0	$97.2	$239.2	$246.6
South Carolina	$417.0	$330.0	$335.8	$340.4
South Dakota	$456.0	$441.1	$239.2	$246.6
Tennessee	$911.0	$554.2	$472.1	$477.0
Texas	$2,821.0	$1,295.1	$1,799.2	$1,828.8
Utah	$543.0	$265.5	$239.2	$246.6
Vermont	$214.0	$189.7	$239.2	$246.6
Virginia	$1,821.0	$975.2	$596.8	$605.4
Washington	$1,199.0	$323.3	$496.3	$503.0
West Virginia	$240.0	$122.2	$239.2	$246.6
Wisconsin	$888.0	$399.0	$440.7	$442.9
Wyoming	$378.0	$373.7	$239.2	$246.6

Source: IRS data are from Cynthia Belmonte, "Tax-Exempt Bonds, 2005," *SOI Bulletin*, Fall 2007, vol. 27, no. 2. The *Bond Buyer* data are from "State Allocations and Use of Private Activity Bonds in 2006," *The Bond Buyer*, June 25, 2007; and "State Allocations and Use of Private Activity Bonds in 2005," *The Bond Buyer*, May 1, 2006.

Table 5 reports the six-year total (2001 to 2006) amount of bonds allocated to selected activities, by state, as reported by the *Bond Buyer*. The total volume capacity is the sum of each year's available capacity. The column marked "Housing" includes bonds issued for (1) mortgages for single family residences, (2) multifamily housing projects, (3) mortgage credit certificates, and (4) other unspecified housing programs. The column labeled "industrial development bonds" (IDBs) is primarily small issue bonds for manufacturing. The *Bond Buyer* "exempt facilities" category includes the following: airports, commuter facilities, docks and wharves, sewer and water facilities, and solid waste disposal facilities. Student loan bonds are used to subsidize loans for qualified students.

The territories (American Samoa, Guam, the Northern Mariana Islands, and the U.S. Virgin Islands) and Puerto Rico also issue bonds for qualified private activities. For the territories with population less than the least populous states, the cap is the population of the territory divided by the population of the least populous state (Wyoming) multiplied by the minimum amount ($262.095 million in 2008).[10]

The "carryforward" and "abandon capacity" columns are important in understanding state allocations. Under current law, states can reserve unused capacity and add the amount to the next year.[11] Capacity can be carried forward up to three years, and states will often use the carry forward to finance large projects that may exceed the *annual* cap. The total accumulated carryforward to 2007 was $22.6 billion for all states and territories. Because the carryforward amount includes allocations from more than one year, the "percent of total" amounts in **Table 6** do not sum to 100%. The District of Columbia allocated the largest carryforward to 2007, 52.5% of the total cap available. The average carryforward was 15.5%.

The last category is abandon capacity. Just as the name implies, abandon capacity is the volume capacity the state did not allocate within three years. For the 2001 to 2006 time period, $3.8 billion was abandon capacity or just 2.6% of all capacity. Delaware abandoned the most, $486.5 million, or approximately 12.7% of the state's available capacity (and about one-fifth of the U.S. total abandon capacity). In contrast, 20 states did not abandon any capacity over the 2001 to 2006 period.

Some could argue that states that abandoned a significant amount of capacity in the past would seem unlikely to change behavior and begin authorizing the use of tax-exempt debt to finance new projects. Alternatively, the newly created range of tax-exempt bonds for new projects may entice states to use capacity that would have otherwise been abandoned. The distribution of abandon capacity could be instructive.

From 2001 to 2006, 20 states and the District of Columbia were subject to the cumulative volume capacity minimum of $1,360.7 million over those six years (see **Table 2**).[12] These are the less populous states where the statutory annual minimum amount was greater than the population based minimum. In these states, the abandon capacity was roughly 5.8% of their capacity ($1.6 billion); the 30 more populous states abandoned considerably less 1.9% of their capacity ($2.2 billion). From these data, it appears the volume cap is relatively less binding for the less populous states; there is "excess capacity" in

these states. Thus, increasing or expanding the amount available for new projects would be relatively less effective in inducing new investment in less populous states relative to more populous states.

Table 5. State Use of Private Activity Bond Volume Cap, 2001 to 2006 (In $ Millions)

State	Total Cap[a]	Housing	IDB — Small Issue	Exempt Facility	Student Loan	Carry-forward to 2007	Abandon Capacity
US Total	**146,000.0**	**73,577.0**	**7,563.0**	**15,492.0**	**21,321.0**	**22,638.0**	**3,818.0**
Alabama	2,036.3	591.4	167.5	135.3	75.0	893.4	68.1
Alaska	1,360.7	645.6	0.0	148.1	279.4	358.0	90.6
Arizona	2,509.0	1,284.2	18.7	424.5	569.8	206.5	82.4
Arkansas	1,360.7	333.2	100.7	247.8	478.5	188.1	176.0
California	15,939.1	10,882.4	248.0	1,416.8	1,047.9	1,315.8	9.9
Colorado	2,043.5	1,679.9	62.3	154.8	493.3	0.0	0.0
Connecticut	1,569.0	1,421.6	23.9	43.3	107.3	36.1	41.1
Delaware	1,360.7	602.7	4.5	15.4	0.0	596.2	486.5
D.C.	1,360.2	486.1	15.0	0.0	0.0	518.8	330.9
Florida	7,658.6	3,332.4	354.2	742.2	984.2	2,377.6	459.5
Georgia	3,909.4	1,982.8	257.1	239.6	0.0	1,130.1	363.0
Hawaii	1,360.7	142.6	0.0	180.0	125.0	575.3	138.4
Idaho	1,360.7	656.8	37.6	58.1	20.0	362.5	0.0
Illinois	5,662.2	2,191.2	504.6	171.1	89.0	n.a.	0.0
Indiana	2,797.0	1,460.0	517.1	641.4	231.7	0.0	0.0
Iowa	1,362.4	749.8	79.5	90.4	268.9	70.4	0.0
Kansas	1,360.7	1,171.3	119.4	38.0	0.0	0.0	0.0
Kentucky	1,859.5	1,054.4	79.5	388.5	530.6	1.0	0.0
Louisiana	2,033.3	669.2	236.5	199.7	472.1	161.8	55.8
Maine	1,360.7	600.6	141.3	0.0	225.0	461.8	3.2
Maryland	2,476.8	1,617.1	83.9	40.6	0.0	698.8	236.3
Massach-usetts	2,897.6	1,494.2	228.1	446.1	873.6	4.0	0.0
Michigan	4,549.4	856.9	307.7	591.1	1,575.1	930.1	16.0
Minnesota	2,280.4	1,781.9	72.6	86.0	197.4	161.4	0.0
Mississippi	1,360.7	503.4	62.0	79.7	326.6	380.1	3.8
Missouri	2,578.1	1,476.6	130.2	205.0	562.9	149.2	21.8
Montana	1,360.7	733.8	3.0	178.0	628.2	208.1	0.0
Nebraska	1,360.7	793.3	107.2	0.0	0.0	500.0	0.0
Nevada	1,360.7	436.9	82.5	119.0	0.0	475.0	32.3
New Hampshire	1,360.7	662.0	38.4	243.0	515.0	86.2	0.0
New Jersey	3,890.9	935.7	272.1	570.8	1,071.0	747.0	433.4

Table 5. (Continued)

State	Total Capa	Housing	IDB — Small Issue	Exempt Facility	Student Loan	Carry-forward to 2007	Abandon Capacity
New Mexico	1,360.7	791.3	23.0	109.7	512.6	65.2	0.0
New York	8,662.5	6,896.0	217.5	111.5	0.0	763.3	0.0
North Carolina	3,791.6	729.8	187.2	544.5	1,407.6	593.5	98.3
North Dakota	1,360.7	694.6	5.1	15.0	1.0	714.7	83.4
Ohio	5,167.9	2,439.7	426.6	524.8	598.4	1,198.5	10.4
Oklahoma	1,583.8	909.1	57.7	218.0	453.7	66.2	22.6
Oregon	1,602.1	806.0	56.3	104.5	0.0	627.3	0.3
Pennsylvania	5,590.3	1,779.4	739.5	1,403.7	970.0	638.4	0.0
Rhode Island	1,360.7	483.0	24.4	100.1	370.1	236.3	0.0
South Carolina	1,850.7	567.2	139.9	355.4	674.7	175.8	66.0
South Dakota	1,360.7	780.0	18.8	0.0	0.0	616.9	214.8
Tennessee	2,637.3	941.1	125.4	262.4	972.3	0.0	0.0
Texas	9,933.6	5,004.7	204.9	2,383.0	1,635.8	707.9	134.7
Utah	1,360.7	632.9	58.5	85.4	506.8	139.6	0.0
Vermont	1,360.7	488.3	17.3	209.2	852.2	27.8	9.0
Virginia	3,321.6	2,235.0	135.1	156.7	0.0	704.3	28.9
Washington	2,762.5	1,579.2	130.1	422.7	428.7	284.2	0.0
West Virginia	1,360.7	509.8	192.8	268.2	0.0	462.5	75.7
Wisconsin	2,469.8	1,311.1	254.3	93.0	0.0	806.6	25.2
Wyoming	1,360.7	768.4	193.0	230.2	190.0	215.7	0.0

Source: Author calculations based on *Bond Buyer* data.

a. Does not include the new volume created by legislation identified in Table 3 of this report.

Table 6. State Use of Private Activity Bond Volume Cap as Percent of Total, 2001 to 2006

State	Housing	IDB — Small Issue	Exempt Facility	Student Loan	Carry-forward to 2007	Abandon Capacity
US Total	50.4%	5.2%	10.6%	14.6%	15.5%	2.6%
Alabama	29.0%	8.2%	6.6%	3.7%	43.9%	3.3%
Alaska	47.4%	0.0%	10.9%	20.5%	26.3%	6.7%
Arizona	51.2%	0.7%	16.9%	22.7%	8.2%	3.3%
Arkansas	24.5%	7.4%	18.2%	35.2%	13.8%	12.9%
California	68.3%	1.6%	8.9%	6.6%	8.3%	0.1%
Colorado	82.2%	3.0%	7.6%	24.1%	0.0%	0.0%

State	Housing	IDB — Small Issue	Exempt Facility	Student Loan	Carry-forward to 2007	Abandon Capacity
Connecticut	90.6%	1.5%	2.8%	6.8%	2.3%	2.6%
Delaware	44.3%	0.3%	1.1%	0.0%	43.8%	35.8%
D.C.	35.7%	1.1%	0.0%	0.0%	38.1%	24.3%
Florida	43.5%	4.6%	9.7%	12.9%	31.0%	6.0%
Georgia	50.7%	6.6%	6.1%	0.0%	28.9%	9.3%
Hawaii	10.5%	0.0%	13.2%	9.2%	42.3%	10.2%
Idaho	48.3%	2.8%	4.3%	1.5%	26.6%	0.0%
Illinois	38.7%	8.9%	3.0%	1.6%	na	0.0%
Indiana	52.2%	18.5%	22.9%	8.3%	0.0%	0.0%
Iowa	55.0%	5.8%	6.6%	19.7%	5.2%	0.0%
Kansas	86.1%	8.8%	2.8%	0.0%	0.0%	0.0%
Kentucky	56.7%	4.3%	20.9%	28.5%	0.1%	0.0%
Louisiana	32.9%	11.6%	9.8%	23.2%	8.0%	2.7%
Maine	44.1%	10.4%	0.0%	16.5%	33.9%	0.2%
Maryland	65.3%	3.4%	1.6%	0.0%	28.2%	9.5%
Massachusetts	51.6%	7.9%	15.4%	30.1%	0.1%	0.0%
Michigan	18.8%	6.8%	13.0%	34.6%	20.4%	0.4%
Minnesota	78.1%	3.2%	3.8%	8.7%	7.1%	0.0%
Mississippi	37.0%	4.6%	5.9%	24.0%	27.9%	0.3%
Missouri	57.3%	5.1%	8.0%	21.8%	5.8%	0.8%
Montana	53.9%	0.2%	13.1%	46.2%	15.3%	0.0%
Nebraska	58.3%	7.9%	0.0%	0.0%	36.7%	0.0%
Nevada	32.1%	6.1%	8.7%	0.0%	34.9%	2.4%
New Hampshire	48.7%	2.8%	17.9%	37.8%	6.3%	0.0%
New Jersey	24.0%	7.0%	14.7%	27.5%	19.2%	11.1%
New Mexico	58.2%	1.7%	8.1%	37.7%	4.8%	0.0%
New York	79.6%	2.5%	1.3%	0.0%	8.8%	0.0%
North Carolina	19.2%	4.9%	14.4%	37.1%	15.7%	2.6%
North Dakota	51.0%	0.4%	1.1%	0.1%	52.5%	6.1%
Ohio	47.2%	8.3%	10.2%	11.6%	23.2%	0.2%
Oklahoma	57.4%	3.6%	13.8%	28.6%	4.2%	1.4%
Oregon	50.3%	3.5%	6.5%	0.0%	39.2%	0.0%
Pennsylvania	31.8%	13.2%	25.1%	17.4%	11.4%	0.0%
Rhode Island	35.5%	1.8%	7.4%	27.2%	17.4%	0.0%
South Carolina	30.6%	7.6%	19.2%	36.5%	9.5%	3.6%

Table 6. (Continued)

State	Housing	IDB — Small Issue	Exempt Facility	Student Loan	Carry-forward to 2007	Abandon Capacity
South Dakota	57.3%	1.4%	0.0%	0.0%	45.3%	15.8%
Tennessee	35.7%	4.8%	9.9%	36.9%	0.0%	0.0%
Texas	50.4%	2.1%	24.0%	16.5%	7.1%	1.4%
Utah	46.5%	4.3%	6.3%	37.2%	10.3%	0.0%
Vermont	35.9%	1.3%	15.4%	62.6%	2.0%	0.7%
Virginia	67.3%	4.1%	4.7%	0.0%	21.2%	0.9%
Washington	57.2%	4.7%	15.3%	15.5%	10.3%	0.0%
West Virginia	37.5%	14.2%	19.7%	0.0%	34.0%	5.6%
Wisconsin	53.1%	10.3%	3.8%	0.0%	32.7%	1.0%
Wyoming	56.5%	14.2%	16.9%	14.0%	15.9%	0.0%

Source: Author calculations based on *Bond Buyer* data.

Note: The carryforward amount includes allocations from more than one year, thus, the "percent of total" amounts do not sum to 100%.

SELECTED PRIVATE ACTIVITY BOND LEGISLATION

Members of the 110th Congress have enacted one private activity bond law and introduced several bills that would change the tax treatment of state and local bonds issued to finance private activities. These activities include housing, economic development, infrastructure investment, renewable energy, recycling, conservation initiatives, and tribal government parity.

Housing Related Proposals

On May 25, 2007, the *U.S. Troop Readiness, Veterans' Care, Katrina Recovery, and Iraq Accountability Appropriations Act* (H.R. 2206, P.L. 110-28) was enacted. The legislation relaxes the tax-exempt mortgage revenue bond rules for repairs and reconstruction of homes in the areas affected by the 2005 Hurricanes Katrina, Rita, and Wilma. The underlying bonds are subject to the volume limits that apply to Qualified Gulf Opportunity Bonds and do not create additional capacity.

The *Katrina Housing Tax Relief Act of 2007* (H.R. 1562) would extend, to the end of 2010, tax-exempt mortgage revenue bonds issued to finance rehabilitation loans for repair and reconstruction of homes in areas devastated by Hurricane Katrina. The legislation passed the House on March 27, 2007, by voice vote. The Senate has not yet acted on the legislation. H.R. 4312 and the related S. 2757 would further expand the Gulf Opportunity Bond provisions.

Two House bills, H.R. 3742 and the *Military Assistance Act of 2007*, H.R. 3816, would eliminate the first-time homebuyer requirement for mortgage revenue bonds issued to finance mortgages for qualified veterans. More generally, H.R. 5720, which was approved by the House Ways and Means Committee on April 9, 2008, would allocate an additional $10 billion for mortgage revenue bonds and residential rental facilities. In addition, a Senate-amended version of H.R. 3221 would also allocate an additional $10 billion.

H.R. 5239 and S. 2517 would allow the issuance of $15 billion in additional mortgage revenue bonds for the purchase of subprime mortgage loans. A related bill, S. 2574, the *Mortgage Refinancing Initiative Act of 2008*, would permit the Secretary of Treasury to allocate an additional $5 million each for 2008 and 2009. (Note that the amount may have been intended to be $5 *billion* for each year.)

Economic Development Proposals

Two companion bills, the *Research and Development Tax Credit Act of 2007* (H.R. 1712) and the *Research Competitiveness Act of 2007* (S. 41), would allow the issuance of tax-exempt facility bonds for research park facilities used in connection with research and experimentation. These bonds would be subject to the existing state volume cap. The tax-exempt bonds created by S. 672 would not be subject to a volume cap. H.R. 3089 would create a new category of private activity bonds for construction of domestic use oil refineries.

Under H.R. 2110, tax-exempt small issue bonds could be used to finance the purchase of property or land used primarily for the processing of agricultural products. These bonds would be subject to the state volume cap. The *Trade and Globalization Assistance Act of 2007*, H.R. 3920, would increase the amount of tax- exempt bond proceeds a project can use in a newly designated "manufacturing zone."

The *Empowerment Zone and Renewal Community Enhancement Act of 2007* (H.R. 2578 and S. 1627) would expand the empowerment zone and enterprise community program by creating "rural enterprise communities." Each community would be subject to an individual volume limit of $200 million, but they would not be subject to the state volume cap. The legislation also does not include a national cap.

Infrastructure Investment Proposals

Two bills would allow bonds that are guaranteed by the federal government and by the quasi-federal home loan bank to also be tax-exempt. Generally, federally guaranteed debt cannot be tax-exempt. H.R. 1959 would permit interest on federally guaranteed water, wastewater, and essential community facilities loans to be tax exempt. H.R. 2091 would allow the federal home loan banks (FHLBs) to guarantee tax-exempt bonds. FHLBs guarantees would likely be used for bonds issued by state and local governments, or private entities acting on behalf of state and local governments, such as water and sewer authorities. In the Senate, S. 1963 would also allow bonds guaranteed by the FHLB to be tax-exempt.

The *Spaceport Equality Act of 2007* (H.R. 2285 and S. 1355) would create a new facility eligible for tax-exempt financing: spaceports. The new bonds would not be subject to the state volume cap as long as the facility is government owned. The tax treatment of the new bonds would be similar to that for airports.

The *Clean Air and Water Investment Act of 2007* (H.R. 2812) would create a new qualified exempt facility: air or water pollution control facilities. The legislation identifies such facilities as those intended "...to abate or control water or atmospheric pollution or contamination by removing, altering, disposing, or storing pollutants, contaminants, wastes, or heat...." The bonds would be subject to the state volume cap.

Environmental and Conservation Proposals

The *Recycling Investment Saves Energy Act* (S. 1587) would allow for the tax- exempt bond financing of qualified recycling facilities. The tax-exempt bonds issued to finance these facilities would be subject to the state volume cap. The *Clean Renewable Energy and Economic Development Incentives Act of 2007* (S. 1531) would expand the list of private activities to include facilities that use renewable resources for energy production. Similarly, the *Rural Community Renewable Energy Bonds Act* (S. 672) would allow the issuance of tax-exempt small issue bonds to finance qualified renewable energy facilities.

The *Community Forestry Conservation Act of 2007* (S. 1952 and H.R. 3456) would allow the issuance of $10 billion in tax-exempt bonds to finance the purchase and conservation of forests by qualified organizations as defined in the legislation. The bonds would be allocated by region and would not be subject to the state volume cap.

S. 1987 would provide an additional $12 billion in private activity bond volume cap for the construction of an alternative motor vehicle facility. The bonds must be issued before January 1, 2013 and a single issuer can use a maximum of $4 billion of capacity.

Other Proposals

The *Tribal Government Tax-Exempt Bond Parity Act of 2007* (H.R. 3164 and S. 1850) would expand the range of activities that tribal governments can use tax- exempt debt to finance. Under current law, tribal governments can use tax-exempt bonds to finance spending on "essential government services," but not other activities. However, no consistent definition of essential government service has been identified. The legislation defines "essential government service" as "... any function which is performed by a State or local government with general taxing powers." Qualified private activities would likely not be included in essential government function under this definition.

End Notes

[1] Technically, private activity bonds that receive tax-exempt status are called *qualified* private activity bonds. For this report, the modifier "qualified" has been dropped.

[2] The $5.6 billion is the sum of each, separate, JCT revenue loss estimate as published in their *General Explanation* documents for each respective Congress. Full citations are available in the sources note for **Table 3** of this report.

[3] Cynthia Belmonte, "Tax-Exempt Bonds, 2005," *SOI Bulletin*, Fall 2007, vol. 27, no. 2.

[4] For more, see CRS Report RL3 1457, *Private Activity Bonds: An Introduction*, by Steven Maguire.

[5] IRS data are all from Cynthia Belmonte, "Tax-Exempt Bonds, 2005," *SOI Bulletin*, Fall 2007, vol. 27, no. 2.

[6] 26 U.S.C. § 143. Mortgage bond proceeds can be applied to the purchase, improvement, or rehabilitation of owner-occupied residences.

[7] For all years except 2004, 21 states and the District were subject to the minimum. In 2004, Iowa was subject to a higher population-based cap.

[8] Current refunding is the practice of issuing bonds to replace existing bonds. Issuers typically do this to "lock-in" lower interest rates or more favorable borrowing terms. Current refunding is allowed as long as the "old" bonds are redeemed within 90 days of the issuance of the refunding bonds. *Advance* refunding is the practice of issuing new bonds to replace existing bonds, but not immediately (within 90 days) retiring the old bonds. Thus, two sets of tax-exempt bonds are outstanding for the same project.

[9] IRS data are from Cynthia Belmonte, "Tax-Exempt Bonds, 2005," SOI Bulletin, Fall 2007, vol. 27, no. 2.

[10] 26 U.S.C. § 146(d)(4).

[11] 26 U.S.C. § 146(f)(3).

In: Private Activity, Tax-Exempt and Tax Credit… ISBN: 978-1-61470-227-6
Editor: Fredrick Kjellson

Chapter 3

TAX-EXEMPT BONDS: A DESCRIPTION OF STATE AND LOCAL GOVERNMENT DEBT

Steven Maguire

SUMMARY

This report provides information about state and local government debt. State and local governments often issue debt instruments in exchange for the use of individuals' and businesses' savings. This debt obligates state and local governments to make interest payments for the use of these savings and to repay, at some time in the future, the amount borrowed. State and local governments finance capital facilities with debt rather than out of current tax revenue in order to match the time pattern of benefits from these capital facilities with the time pattern of tax payments.

The federal government subsidizes the cost of most state and local debt by excluding the interest income from federal income taxation. This tax exemption of interest income is granted because it is believed that state and local capital facilities will be under provided if state and local taxpayers have to pay the full cost.

State and local debt is issued as bonds, to be repaid over a period of time greater than one year and perhaps exceeding 20 years, and as notes, to be repaid within one year. General obligation bonds are secured by the promise to repay with general tax revenue, and revenue bonds are secured with the promise to use the stream of revenue generated by the facility built with the bond proceeds. Most debt is issued to finance new capital facilities, but some is issued to refund a prior bond issue (usually to take advantage of lower interest rates). Tax-exempt bonds issued for some activities are classified as governmental bonds and can be issued without federal constraint because most of the benefits from the capital facilities are enjoyed by the general public. Many tax-exempt revenue bonds are issued for activities Congress has classified as private because most of the benefits from the activities appear to be enjoyed by private individuals and businesses. The annual volume of a subset of these tax-exempt private-activity bonds is capped.

Arbitrage bonds devote a substantial share of the proceeds to the purchase of assets with higher interest rates than that being paid on the tax-exempt bonds. Such arbitrage bonds are not tax exempt because Congress does not want state and local governments to issue tax-exempt bonds and use the proceeds to earn arbitrage profits. The arbitrage profits could substitute for state and local taxes.

The major policy issue in this area is the effort to use tax-exempt bonds to increase federal financial support for a variety of public facilities. Another policy issue is whether constraints should be relaxed on the types of activities for which state and local governments can issue tax-exempt debt. The extent to which the current arbitrage bond rules prohibit what some consider legitimate state and local financial behavior is a related area of dispute. The list of activities that classify tax- exempt private-activity bonds — and whether they should be included in the volume cap — is another area of controversy. This report will be updated as new data become available.

WHAT IS DEBT?

Individuals and businesses lend their accumulated savings to borrowers. In exchange, borrowers give lenders a debt instrument. These debt instruments, typically called bonds, represent a promise by borrowers to pay interest income to lenders on the principal (the amount of money borrowed) until the principal is repaid to the lenders. This principal, sometimes called the proceeds, generally is used to finance the construction of capital facilities.

Why Do State and Local Governments Issue Debt?

Since public capital facilities provide services over a long period of time, it makes financial and economic sense to pay for the facilities over a similarly long period of time. This is particularly true for state and local governments. Their taxpayers lay claim to the benefits from these facilities by dint of residency and relinquish their claim to benefits when they move. Given the demands a market-oriented society places on labor mobility, taxpayers are reluctant to pay today for state and local capital services to be received in the future. The rational response of the state or local official concerned with satisfying the preferences of constituents is to match the timing of the payments to the flow of services, precisely the function served by long-term bond financing. An attempt to pay for capital facilities "up front" is likely to result in a less than optimal rate of public capital formation.

State and local governments are also faced with the necessity of planning their budget for the year (or in some cases for two years). This requires a balancing of revenue forecasts against forecasts of the demand for services and spending. Not infrequently, the inevitable unforeseen circumstances that undermine any forecast cause a revenue shortfall, which must be financed with short-term borrowing, or "notes." In addition, even when the forecasts are met, the timing of expenditures may precede the arrival of revenues, creating the necessity to borrow within an otherwise balanced fiscal year. Finally, temporarily high interest rates that prevail at the time bonds are issued to finance a capital project may induce short-term borrowing in anticipation of a drop in rates. ignored the nineteenth century legacy of unrealistically restrictive constitutional and statutory limitations on state and local borrowing.[1]

What Makes State and Local Debt Special?

The federal government has chosen to intervene in the public capital market by granting the debt instruments of state and local governments a unique privilege — the exemption of interest income earned on these bonds from federal income tax. The tax exemption lowers the cost of capital for state and local governments, which should then induce an increase in state and local capital formation. The lower cost of capital arises because investors would be indifferent between taxable bonds (e.g., corporate bonds) that yield a 10% rate of return before taxes and tax-exempt bonds of equivalent risk that yield a 6.5% return. The taxable bond interest earnings carry a tax liability (35% of the interest income in most cases) making the after tax return on the two bonds identical at 6.5%. Thus, state and local governments could raise capital from investors at an interest cost 3.5 percentage points (350 basis points) lower than a borrower issuing taxable debt.

Table 1. Yield on Tax-Exempt and Corporate Bonds of Equivalent Risk, the Yield Spread, and the Yield Ratio: 1980 to 2007

Year	High Grade Tax-Exempt Yield (%)	AAA Corporate Yield (%)	Yield Spread (%)	Yield Ratio (tax-exempt/ corporate)
1980	8.51	11.94	3.43	0.71
1981	11.23	14.17	2.94	0.79
1982	11.57	13.79	2.22	0.84
1983	9.47	12.04	2.57	0.79
1984	10.15	12.71	2.56	0.80
1985	9.18	11.37	2.19	0.81
1986	7.38	9.02	1.64	0.82
1987	7.73	9.38	1.65	0.82
1988	7.76	9.71	1.95	0.80
1989	7.24	9.26	2.02	0.78
1990	7.25	9.32	2.07	0.78
1991	6.89	8.77	1.88	0.79
1992	6.41	8.14	1.73	0.79
1993	5.63	7.22	1.59	0.78
1994	6.19	7.96	1.77	0.78
1995	5.95	7.59	1.64	0.78
1996	5.75	7.37	1.62	0.78
1997	5.55	7.26	1.71	0.76
1998	5.12	6.53	1.41	0.78
1999	5.43	7.04	1.61	0.77
2000	5.77	7.62	1.85	0.76
2001	5.19	7.08	1.89	0.73
2002	5.05	6.49	1.44	0.78
2003	4.73	5.67	0.94	0.83

Year	High Grade Tax-Exempt Yield (%)	AAA Corporate Yield (%)	Yield Spread (%)	Yield Ratio (tax-exempt/ corporate)
2004	4.63	5.63	1.00	0.82
2005	4.29	5.24	0.95	0.82
2006	4.42	5.59	1.17	0.79
2007	4.42	5.52	1.10	0.80

Source: Council of Economic Advisors, *Economic Report of the President*, February 2008, Table B-73.

Generally, the degree to which tax-exempt debt is favored is measured in two ways. The yield spread is the difference between interest rate on corporate bonds and the interest rate on municipal bonds of equivalent risk. **Table 1** lists the average yield on high-grade municipal bonds and AAA-rated corporate bonds from 1980 to 2007, and the corresponding yield spread. The spread grew to a high of 3.43% in 1980 and dropped to a low of 0.94% in 2003. The greater the yield spread, the greater is the nominal savings to state and local governments as measured by the interest rates they would have to pay if they financed with taxable debt. As the spread approaches zero, state and local borrowing costs approach the level of taxable bond interest rates.

Another measure, the yield ratio (which is an average rate on tax-exempt bonds divided by an average rate on a corporate bond of like term and risk), adjusts the spread for the level of interest rates. The lower the ratio, the greater the savings to state and local governments relative to taxable debt. As the ratio approaches one, the cost of tax-exempt state and local borrowing approaches that of taxable borrowing. As shown in **Table 1**, the ratio was lowest in 1980 at 0.71 and reached a peak of 0.84 in 1982. For the last decade the ratio has been relatively stable.

These variations in the cost of state and local borrowing relative to the cost of taxable borrowing depend upon the demand for and supply of both tax-exempt and taxable bonds. Demand for tax-exempt bonds depends upon the number of investors, their wealth, statutory tax rates, and alternative investment opportunities. Supply depends upon the desire of the state and local sector for capital facilities and their ability to engage in conduit financing (issuing state or local government bonds and passing the proceeds through to businesses or individuals for their private use). Almost all of the factors which influence demand and supply are affected by federal tax policy.

Table 2. Tax Expenditure on the Outstanding Stock of Public Purpose Tax-Exempt Bonds: 1994 to 2007 (in Billions)

Year	Tax Expenditure	Year	Tax Expenditure
1994	$19.6	2001	$27.4
1995	$20.4	2002	$29.9
1996	$24.9	2003	$31.1
1997	$19.9	2004	$26.2
1998	$24.6	2005	$26.4
1999	$27.5	2006	$23.0
2000	$26.8	2007	$23.5

Source: Office of Management and Budget. *Analytical Perspectives: Budget of the United States Government*, various years.

WHAT DOES TAX EXEMPTION COST THE FEDERAL GOVERNMENT?

The direct cost to the federal government of this interest exclusion is the individual and corporate income tax revenue forgone. Consider a 35% marginal tax rate corporate investor who purchases a 6.5% tax-exempt bond with principal of $1,000 that is to be repaid after 20 years. Each year for 20 years this taxpayer receives $65 in tax-exempt interest income. Each year the federal government forgoes collecting $35 of revenue because the revenue loss is based upon the yield the taxpayer forgoes. For example, if the investor had purchased a taxable bond carrying a 10% interest rate, he would have received $100 in interest income and paid $35 in income taxes on that income.[2]

The annual federal revenue loss (or tax expenditure) on the outstanding stock of tax-exempt bonds is reported in the *Analytical Perspectives* section of the Budget every year. The estimates for the last 14 years are displayed in **Table 2.**[3] Because they are based upon the outstanding stock of public-purpose tax-exempt bonds, it takes time for some legislative changes to show up in these data. The amount of forgone tax revenue from the exclusion of interest income on public-purpose tax- exempt bonds is substantial, $23.5 billion in 2007.

WHY DOES THE FEDERAL GOVERNMENT SUBSIDIZE STATE AND LOCAL DEBT?

When first introduced in 1913, the federal income tax excluded the interest income earned by holders of the debt obligations of states and their political subdivisions from taxable income. It was asserted by many that any taxation of this interest income would be unconstitutional because the exemption was protected by the Tenth Amendment and the doctrine of intergovernmental tax immunity. The U.S. Supreme Court rejected this claim of constitutional protection in 1988 in *South Carolina v. Baker* (485 U.S. 505, [1988]).

Although the legal basis for the subsidy is statutory rather than constitutional, the policy reason for the subsidy is economic. Economic theory suggests that certain types of goods and services will not be provided in the correct or "optimal" amounts by the private sector because some of the benefits are consumed collectively, a street light for example. The Nation's welfare can be increased by public provision of these goods and services, and some of these public goods and services are best provided by state or local governments. However, some of the goods and services provided by state or local governments benefit both residents, who pay taxes, and nonresidents, who pay minimal if any taxes. Since state and local taxpayers are likely to be unwilling to provide these services to nonresidents without compensation, it is probable that state and local services will be under provided. In theory, the cost reduction provided by the exemption of interest income compensates state and local taxpayers for benefits provided to nonresidents and encourages these governments to provide the optimal amount of public services.

CLASSIFYING STATE AND LOCAL DEBT INSTRUMENTS

State and local debt can be classified based on (1) the *maturity* (or term), which is the length of time before the principal is repaid; (2) the *type of security*, which is the financial backing for the debt; (3) the *use of the proceeds* for either new facilities or to refinance previously-issued bonds; and (4) whether the *type of activity* being financed has a public or a private purpose. Another important factor is the level risk. Just about every bond issued by a state or local government is rated based on the probability of default. The privately managed rating agencies incorporate all of the above factors as well as the financial health of the entity issuing the bonds when arriving upon a bond rating. The higher the default risk, the lower the rating.

Maturity: Short-Term vs. Long-Term

Tax and Revenue Anticipation Notes

State and local governments must borrow money for long periods of time and for short periods of time. Long-term debt instruments are usually referred to as bonds, and carry maturities in excess of one year. Short-term debt instruments are usually referred to as notes, and carry maturities of 12 months or less. If the notes are to be paid from specific taxes due in the near future, they usually are called tax anticipation notes (TANs); if from anticipated intergovernmental revenue, they are called revenue anticipation notes (RANs). If the notes are to be paid from long-term borrowing (e.g., bonds), they are called bond anticipation notes (BANs). Tax anticipation notes and revenue anticipation notes are often grouped together and referred to as tax and revenue anticipation notes (TRANs). **Table 3** displays the volume of long-term and short- term borrowing since 1980. Long-term borrowing dominates state and local debt activity in most years, with the long-term share peaking in 1985 at over 90% of this market.

Auction Rate Securities

Auction Rate Securities (ARSs) are long-term debt obligations with the unique feature of adjustable or variable interest rates. In contrast to long-term, fixed rate securities, issuers go to auction periodically (anywhere from every 7 to 35 days) to reset the interest rate on the debt outstanding. The auction mechanism and interest rate parameters vary by issuer (and issue) though most use what is termed a "Dutch auction" where each bidder submits a bid for the amount they are willing to purchase at a given interest rate. All bids are ordered from lowest interest rate to highest interest rate and the rate where the market clears, e.g., where all bonds would be purchased, establishes the new ARS rate. All bidders receive that rate.

Unique Features of ARSs

ARSs typically have a "call option" where the issuer can buy the ARS back at par (face value) at any scheduled auction and then retire the debt. Most ARSs are insured by the issuer because they *do not* carry a "put" option that would allow bondholders to sell the bonds at a specified price to the issuer or a designated third party. The bond insurance reduces risk and thus interest rate making the bonds less costly to issuers. For this reason, ARSs are

> very sensitive to changes in credit ratings and normally require the highest ratings (e.g. AAA/Aaa) to make them marketable. This is usually achieved with bond insurance.[4]

Table 3. Volume of State and Local Tax-Exempt Debt: 1980 to 2007

Year	Short-Term (in millions)	Long-Term (in millions)	Long-Term Share of Total
1980	$26,485	$47,133	64.0%
1981	$34,443	$46,134	57.3%
1982	$43,390	$77,179	64.0%
1983	$35,849	$83,348	69.9%
1984	$31,068	$101,882	76.6%
1985	$20,809	$206,991	90.9%
1986	$22,046	$150,638	87.2%
1987	$20,518	$105,027	83.7%
1988	$23,666	$117,316	83.2%
1989	$29,596	$125,005	80.9%
1990	$34,804	$127,828	78.6%
1991	$44,800	$172,443	79.4%
1992	$42,894	$234,667	84.5%
1993	$47,354	$292,249	86.1%
1994	$40,293	$165,034	80.4%
1995	$38,346	$159,983	80.7%
1996	$41,695	$185,014	81.6%
1997	$46,434	$220,672	82.6%
1998	$34,584	$286,817	89.2%
1999	$36,511	$227,741	86.2%
2000	$41,249	$200,880	83.0%
2001	$56,610	$288,083	83.6%
2002	$72,386	$358,569	83.2%
2003	$69,771	$383,498	84.6%
2004	$56,951	$359,695	86.3%
2005	$50,544	$408,193	89.0%
2006	$44,126	$388,656	89.8%
2007	$57,999	$429,727	88.1%

Source: *The Bond Buyer Yearbook*, 2007 and earlier editions.

A Failed Auction

The existing holders of ARSs offer bids as well as new bidders. If all bids of both existing bond holders and new participants fail to clear the market, the auction is termed a "failed auction." In this scenario, the original agreement with bondholder stipulates a "reservation" interest rate the issuer must pay in the event of a failed auction at least until the next successful auction. The reservation rate is typically significantly higher than current market interest rates. Because the rate is higher than market interest rates, issuers of ARSs wish to avoid paying the reservation rate.

Growth of ARSs

The issuance of ARSs has grown considerably in the last 20 years. In 1988, the Bond Buyer identified one ARS issue valued at $25 million; none were issued in 1987.[5] In 2004, the peak year, 438 ARS bonds valued at $42.5 billion were issued. The number of ARSs issues has since dropped to 322 and $38.7 billion in 2007.

Security: General Obligation, Revenue, and Lease Rental Bonds

Another important characteristic of tax-exempt bonds is the security provided to the bondholder. General obligation (GO) bonds pledge the full faith and credit of the issuing government. The issuing government makes an unconditional pledge to use its powers of taxation to honor its liability for interest and principal repayment. Revenue bonds, or non-guaranteed debt, pledge only the earnings from revenue- producing activities, most often the earnings from the facilities being financed with the revenue bonds. Should these earnings prove to be inadequate to honor these commitments, the issuing government is under no obligation to use its taxing powers to finance the shortfall. Some revenue bonds are issued with credit enhancements provided by insurance or bank letters of credit that guarantee payment upon such a revenue shortfall.

The first two columns of **Table 4** display the breakdown between long-term GO and revenue bonds since 1980. The long-term market has been and continues to be dominated by revenue bonds, which are nonguaranteed debt instruments. During the 1960s (not shown in this table), revenue bonds constituted less than 40% of longterm bond volume; during the 1970s (also not shown) the revenue bond share crept into the 50% to 65% range; and beginning in 1979 this share settled into the high 60s and low 70s, achieving a high of 73.1% in 1988. The revenue bond share has remained at or just below 70% from 1989 through 2007.

All tax-exempt interest income attributable to state and local governments does not appear in the form of bonds. Governments may engage in installment purchase contracts and finance leases for which the portion of the installment or lease payment to a vendor is tax exempt. For example, computer equipment or road building equipment could be leased from a vendor using a rental agreement or an installment sales contract. Under this type of agreement, the monthly payments to the vendor are large enough to cover the vendor's interest expense on the funds borrowed to purchase the equipment which was leased to the government. This portion that is attributable to interest income is not included in the vendors taxable income. Such transactions are often referred to as municipal leasing.

Lease rental revenue bonds and certificates are variations on revenue bonds. An authority or nonprofit corporation issues bonds, builds a facility with the proceeds, and leases the facility to a municipality. Security for the bonds or certificates is based on the lease payments. When the bonds are retired, the facility belongs to the lessee (the municipality). An advantage to this type of arrangement is that many states' constitutional and statutory definitions do not consider this type of financing to be debt because the lease payments are annual operating expenses based upon appropriated monies.

The leasing technique has also been used to provide tax-exempt funds to nonprofit organizations. A municipality issues the bonds for the construction of a facility that is leased to a nonprofit hospital or university. Again, security for the bonds is based on the lease payments.

Use of the Proceeds: New-Issue vs. Refunding Bonds

Long-term tax-exempt bond issues also can be characterized by their status as new issues or refunding issues. New issues represent bonds issued to finance new capital facilities. Refundings usually are made to replace outstanding bonds with bonds that carry lower interest rates or other favorable terms. As such, the refunding bonds usually do not add to the stock of outstanding bonds or the capital stock. The proceeds of the refunding bonds are used to pay off the remaining principal of the original bond issue, which is retired. Advance refunding bonds, however, do add to the outstanding stock of bonds without adding to the stock of capital. Advance refunding bonds are issued prior to the date on which the original bonds are refunded, so that for a period of time there are two bond issues outstanding to finance the same capital facilities.

Table 4. Volume of Long-Term Tax-Exempt Debt: General Obligation (GO), Revenue, and Refunding Bonds, 1980 to 2007 (in Millions).

Year	Long-Term Bond Volume			Refunding Bonds	
	General Obligation	Revenue	Revenue Share	Amount	Refunding Share
1980	$16,347	$30,786	65.3%	$1,649	3.5%
1981	$13,988	$32,146	69.7%	$1,192	2.6%
1982	$23,276	$53,903	69.8%	$4,044	5.2%
1983	$22,584	$60,764	72.9%	$13,048	15.7%
1984	$27,508	$74,374	73.0%	$11,390	11.2%
1985	$55,287	$148,994	72.9%	$57,867	28.3%
1986	$45,555	$105,417	69.8%	$56,063	37.1%
1987	$30,867	$74,656	70.7%	$38,490	36.5%
1988	$31,502	$85,509	73.1%	$36,591	31.3%
1989	$38,501	$86,504	69.2%	$28,842	23.1%
1990	$40,303	$87,526	68.5%	$19,881	15.6%
1991	$57,110	$115,334	66.9%	$41,444	24.0%
1992	$80,479	$154,188	65.7%	$92,446	39.4%
1993	$91,555	$200,694	68.7%	$150,152	51.4%
1994	$55,767	$109,267	66.2%	$38,601	23.4%
1995	$60,367	$99,615	62.3%	$33,850	21.2%
1996	$64,344	$120,670	65.2%	$45,941	24.8%
1997	$72,297	$148,201	67.2%	$60,161	27.3%
1998	$93,644	$193,031	67.3%	$81,957	28.6%
1999	$71,046	$156,695	68.8%	$38,330	16.8%
2000	$66,573	$134,308	66.9%	$19,587	9.8%
2001	$101,652	$186,431	64.7%	$64,699	22.5%
2002	$125,675	$232,894	65.0%	$92,350	25.8%
2003	$142,767	$240,731	62.8%	$95,240	24.8%
2004	$129,527	$230,168	64.0%	$88,276	24.5%
2005	$144,170	$264,023	64.7%	$130,877	32.1%
2006	$114,858	$273,798	70.4%	$79,163	20.4%
2007	$131,676	$298,051	69.4%	$75,654	17.6%

Source: *The Bond Buyer Yearbook*, 2007 and earlier editions.

Table 5. Private-Activity Bond Volume by Type of Activity in 2005 and 2006.

Private Activity	Issued in (in millions)		Portion of Available Capacity	
	2005	2006	2005	2006
Total Volume Capacity Available	$49,142	$48,675	100.0%	100.0%
New Volume Capacity	$26,079	$26,438	53.1%	54.3%
Carryforward from Previous Years	$23,063	$23,277	46.9%	47.8%
Carryforward to Next Year	$26,337	$22,638	53.6%	46.5%
Single-family Mortgage Revenue	$6,507	$10,093	13.2%	20.7%
Multi-family Housing	$5,562	$6,252	11.3%	12.8%
Student Loans	$5,124	$4,018	10.4%	8.3%
Exempt Facilities	$1,915	$2,605	3.9%	5.4%
Abandon Capacity	$910	$1,417	1.9%	2.9%
Industrial Development	$1,000	$1,195	2.0%	2.5%
Housing not Classified	$822	$562	1.7%	1.2%
Mortgage Credit Certificates	$493	$510	1.0%	1.0%
Other Activities	$485	$284	1.0%	0.6%

Source: "State Allocations of Private-Activity Bonds in 2005," *The Bond Buyer*, May 1, 2006; and "State Allocations and Use of Private-Activity Bonds in 2006," *The Bond Buyer*, June 25, 2007.

The last two columns of **Table 4** show the dollar value of refunding issues and their share of total long-term bond volume. The share varies widely, depending to a great extent on changes in the relative magnitudes of taxable and tax-exempt interest rates. Note that the 1993 increase in the top marginal individual income tax rates may have increased the demand for tax-exempt bonds. Higher tax rates make tax-exempt bonds more attractive relative to taxable bonds, all other things being equal. The increased demand and accompanying lower interest rates may have prompted state and local governments to replace outstanding issues with refunding bonds that carried lower interest rates. In contrast, refundings dropped considerably in 1999 and 2000. The decline could have been in response to higher interest rates or to strong economic conditions in most states which minimized the need for debt finance generally. The story is reversed from 2001 to 2003 as the economy slowed and state budgets were strained by lower tax revenue collections. New issues in 2003 were more than double the amount of new issues in 2000. In

2005, GO bonds and refunding bond volume peaked, likely reflecting the historically low interest rates on tax-exempt debt (see **Table 1**).

Public Purpose vs. Private Purpose

An important characteristic of tax-exempt bonds is the purpose or activity for which the bonds are issued. Most of the tax legislation pertaining to tax-exempt bonds over the last 30 years reflects an effort to restrict tax exemption to bonds issued for activities that satisfy some broadly defined "public" purpose, that is, for which federal taxpayers are likely to receive substantial benefits. Bonds are considered to be for a public purpose if they satisfy either of two criteria: less than 10% of the proceeds are used directly or indirectly by a non-governmental entity; or less than 10% of the bond proceeds are secured directly or indirectly by property used in a trade or business. Bonds that satisfy either of these tests are termed "governmental" bonds and can be issued without federal limit. Bonds that fail both of these tests are termed "private-activity" bonds (PABs) because they provide significant benefits to private individuals or businesses. These projects are ineligible for tax-exempt financing.

Activities which fail the two tests but are considered to provide both public and private benefits have been termed eligible or *qualified* PABs. These selected activities can be financed with tax-exempt bonds. **Table 5** provides the dollar value of new issues of tax-exempt private-activity bonds and their share of total private- activity volume capacity for 2005 and 2006. **Table 6** provides historical data on the portion of PAB volume to total bond volume.

Private Activities Eligible for Tax Exemption

All tax-exempt private-activity bonds are subject to restrictions that do not apply to governmental bonds, chief among them being no advance refundings and the inclusion of the interest income in the alternative minimum income tax base. In addition, the annual dollar value of all bonds issued for most of these activities by all governmental units within a state is limited to the greater of $85 per resident or $262.095 million in 2008. The cap has been adjusted for inflation since 2004. The annual volume cap applies to the total of bonds issued primarily for but not limited to multi- and single-family housing, industrial development, exempt facilities,[6] student loans, and bond-financed takeovers of investor owned utilities (usually electric utilities).

Bonds issued for several activities classified as private are not subject to the volume cap if the facilities are governmentally owned.[7] These activities are airports, docks, and wharves; nonprofit organization facilities; high-speed inter-urban rail facilities; and solid waste disposal facilities that produce electric energy. **Table 7** below reports the estimated tax expenditure for selected private activities that qualify for financing with tax-exempt debt.

Table 6. New-Money, Long-Term Private-Activity Bond Volume as Percent of Total Bond Volume, 1988 to 2005

Year	Total Bond Volume (in millions)	Private Activity Bond (in millions)	Percent of Total Volume
1988	$119,367.8	$29,365.1	24.6%
1989	$125,530.5	$27,650.2	22.0%
1990	$128,045.8	$31,426.0	24.5%
1991	$173,071.5	$27,809.6	16.1%
1992	$235,413.1	$26,868.0	11.4%
1993	$293,052.2	$21,230.6	7.2%
1994	$165,101.3	$25,054.9	15.2%
1995	$161,817.1	$27,942.7	17.3%
1996	$185,207.4	$31,262.0	16.9%
1997	$220,671.7	$37,550.0	17.0%
1998	$286,816.9	$46,288.0	16.1%
1999	$227,740.5	$47,408.0	20.8%
2000	$200,880.0	$41,392.0	20.6%
2001	$288,082.9	$49,356.0	17.1%
2002	$358,568.6	$50,248.0	14.0%
2003	$383,559.3	$45,633.0	11.9%
2004	$359,717.2	$47,877.0	13.3%
2005	$408,260.0	$54,691.0	13.4%

Sources: The 1988 to 1995 data are from Nutter, Sarah, "Tax-Exempt Private Activity Bonds, 1988-1995," *SOI Bulletin*, Summer 1999; Belmonte, Cynthia, "Tax-Exempt Bonds, 2003-2004,: *SOI Bulletin*, Fall 2006 ; and Belmonte, Cynthia, "Tax-Exempt Bonds, 2005, *SOI Bulletin*, Fall 2007. Total long-term bond volume data are from the *Bond Buyer Yearbook 2007*.

Table 7. Federal Tax Expenditure for Selected Private Activities Financed with Tax-Exempt Bonds

Private Activity	2007 Tax Expenditure (in millions)	Percentage of Total
Total of Selected Activities	*$8,310*	*100.00%*
Energy Facilities	$30	0.36%
Water, Sewerage, and Hazardous Waste Disposal	$370	4.45%
Small-Issues	$350	4.21%
Owner-Occupied Mortgage Subsidy	$900	10.83%
Rental Housing	$830	9.99%
Airports, Docks, and Similar Facilities	$850	10.23%
Student Loans	$440	5.29%
Private Nonprofit Educational Facilities	$1,750	21.06%
Hospital Construction	$2,760	33.21%
Veterans' Housing	$30	0.36%

Source: Office of Management and Budget. *Analytical Perspectives: Budget of the United States Government*, Fiscal Year 2009, Table 19-1, pp. 287-291.

Recently, Congress has further expanded the types of private activities eligible for tax-exempt financing and has increased the capacity for selected activities and issuers. A brief description of legislation that Congress has enacted since 2001 follows below.

Economic Growth and Tax Relief Reconciliation Act of 2001

As part of the Economic Growth and Tax Relief Reconciliation Act of 2001 (P.L. 107-16), a new type of tax-exempt private-activity bond was created beginning on January 1, 2002.[8] The act expanded the definition of "an exempt facility bond" to include bonds issued for qualified public educational facilities. Bonds issued for qualified educational facilities are not counted against a state's private-activity volume cap. However, the qualified public educational facility bonds have their own volume capacity limit equal to the greater of $10 multiplied by the State population or $5 million. Since nearly all states would be better off with the $10 per capita limit, the potential new debt would have been approximately $2.8 billion in 2001 if the bonds were available in 2001.

Job Creation and Worker Assistance Act of 2002

The JCWA 2002 (P.L. 107-147) created the New York Liberty Zone (NYLZ) in the wake of the September 11, 2001, terrorist attacks. The legislation included several tax benefits for the NYLZ intended to foster economic revitalization within the NYLZ. Specifically, the so-called "Liberty Bond" program allows New York State (in conjunction and coordination with New York City) to issue up to $8 billion of tax- exempt private-activity bonds for qualified facilities in the NYLZ. Qualified facilities follow the exempt facility rules within section 142 of the IRC. The original deadline to issue the bonds was January 1, 2005, but was extended to January 1, 2010, by P.L. 108-311.

American Jobs Creation Act

In 2004, the American Jobs Creation Act (P.L. 108-3 57) created bonds for "qualified green building and sustainable design projects." The bonds are exempt from the state volume cap and are instead limited to an aggregate of $2 billion for bonds issued between January 1, 2005 and October 1, 2009.

The Safe, Accountable, Flexible, Efficient, Transportation Equity Act of 2005

This legislation created a new type of tax-exempt private activity bond for the construction of rail to highway (or highway to rail) transfer facilities. The national limit is $15 billion and the bonds are not subject to state volume caps for private activity bonds. The Secretary of Transportation allocates the bond authority on a project-by-project basis.

Gulf Opportunity Zone Act of 2005

The hurricanes that struck the Gulf region in late summer 2005, prompted Congress to create a tax-advantaged economic development zone intended to encourage investment and rebuilding in the Gulf region. The Gulf Opportunity Zone, (GOZ), is comprised of the counties where the Federal Emergency Management Agency (FEMA) declared the inhabitants to be eligible for individual and public assistance. Based on proportion of state personal income, the Katrina-affected portion of the GOZ represents approximately 73%of Louisiana's economy, 69% of Mississippi's, and 18% of Alabama's.[9]

Specifically, the "Gulf Opportunity Zone Act of 2005" (GOZA 2005, P.L. 109- 135) contains two provisions that would expand the amount of private-activity bonds outstanding and language to relax the eligibility rules for mortgage revenue bonds. The most significant is the provision to increase the volume cap (see **Table 3**) for private-activity bonds issued for Hurricane Katrina recovery in Alabama, Louisiana, and Mississippi (identified as the Gulf Opportunity Zone, or "GO Zone"). GOZA 2005 would add $2,500 per person in the federally declared Katrina disaster areas in which the residents qualify for individual and public assistance.

The increased volume capacity would add approximately $2.2 billion for Alabama, $7.8 billion for Louisiana, and $4.8 billion for Mississippi in aggregate over the next five years. The legislation defines "qualified project costs" that can be financed with the bond proceeds as (1) the cost of any qualified residential rental project (26 sec. 142(d)); and (2) the cost of acquisition, construction, reconstruction, and renovation of — (i) nonresidential real property (including fixed improvements associated with such property) and (ii) public utility property (26 sec. 1 68(i)(10)), in the GOZ. The additional capacity would have to be issued before January 1, 2011. The provision is estimated to cost $1.556 billion over the 2006-2015 budget window.[10]

The second provision allows for advance refunding of certain tax-exempt bonds. Under GOZA 2005, governmental bonds issued by Alabama, Louisiana, and Mississippi may be advance refunded an additional time and exempt facility private-activity bonds for airports, docks, and wharves once. Private-activity bonds are otherwise not eligible for advance refunding (see earlier discussion of advance refunding).

WHAT ARE ARBITRAGE BONDS?

Many individuals and businesses make money by engaging in arbitrage, borrowing money at one interest rate and lending that borrowed money to others at a higher interest rate. The difference between the rate at which one borrows and the rate at which one lends produces arbitrage earnings. At its most basic level, it is the primary activity of commercial banks — pay depositors an interest rate of "x" and use the deposits to make commercial, automobile, and home loans at "x + y" interest rate. In this context, arbitrage is a time-honored and appropriate financial market activity.

That is not the case in the tax-exempt bond market. State and local governments do not pay federal income tax, and absent federal constraint, have unlimited capacity to issue debt at low interest rates and reinvest the bond proceeds in higher-yielding taxable debt instruments, thereby earning arbitrage profits. Unchecked, state and local governments could substitute arbitrage earnings for a substantial portion of their own citizens' tax effort.

Congress has decided that such arbitrage should be limited, and that tax-exempt bond proceeds must be used as quickly as possible to pay contractors for the construction of the capital facilities for which the bonds were issued. Since it is impossible for bonds to be issued precisely when contractors must be paid for their expenses incurred in building public capital facilities, the tax law provides a three-year period to spend an increasing share of the bond proceeds. Bond issues that have unspent proceeds in excess of the allowed amounts during this three-year spend-down schedule must rebate any arbitrage earnings to the Department of the Treasury. Bond issues are considered to be taxable arbitrage bonds if a governmental unit, in violation of the arbitrage restriction in the tax code, invested a substantial portion of the proceeds "to acquire higher yielding investments, or to replace funds which were used directly or indirectly to acquire higher yielding investments."[11]

WHAT ARE TAX CREDIT BONDS?

The 1997 Taxpayer Relief Act created a new category of tax preferred state and local bonds, the qualified zone academy bond (QZAB) for renovating public school facilities. Congress authorized QZAB debt of $400 million a year for 1998 through 2005 or $3.2 billion over the eight years. The annual limit is allocated among the states in proportion to their share of all individuals below the poverty line.[12]

In 2005, Congress created two new types of tax credit bonds called Clean Renewable Energy Bonds (CREBs) and Gulf Tax Credit Bonds (GTCBs). CREBs were created with the enactment of the Energy Policy Act of 2005, P.L. 109-58.[13] The bonds are intended to encourage the development of renewable energy sources. As with QZABs, purchasers of CREBs receive federal tax credits in lieu of interest payments, and the borrower only repays the principal. The total CREB bond volume is limited to $800 million nationally, and the bonds must be issued before January 1, 2008. Only $500 million may be allocated to qualified projects of qualified borrowers "...which are governmental bodies."[14] In addition, a third party must spend at least 10% of the proceeds of the issue for the bond to qualify. The third party would likely be a private business or individual that would benefit from the CREB expenditures.

After Hurricane Katrina, Congress created yet another tax credit bond called Gulf Tax Credit Bonds (GTCBs). These tax credit bonds are different from the others in that the maturity is capped at two years, and only three states can issue a limited amount: Alabama ($50 million), Louisiana ($200 million), and Mississippi ($100 million). The tax credit rate will approximate the interest rate on equivalent two-year taxable securities. In addition, GTCBs require an equal match from the issuing state. The proceeds from the bonds can be used to pay principal, interest, or premiums on state governmental bonds or make loans to any political subdivision of the state to then be used to pay principal, interest, or premiums on the political subdivision's governmental bonds. The bonds can only be issued in 2006.

The subsidy for tax credit bonds is not provided in the form of the exemption of interest income from federal income tax, as is true for tax-exempt bonds, including bonds issued for public elementary and secondary education facilities. Rather, the subsidy for them is a credit taken by eligible financial institutions against the federal taxes they owe. The credit rate is calculated by the Treasury Department such that the bonds can be issued without discount and without any interest cost to the issuer. Unlike QZABs, where issuers are chosen by the state, issuers of CREBs are selected by the Secretary of Treasury. For GTCBs, the governor of the issuing state designates the use of the bond proceeds.

Table 8. Comparison of Three Types of Bonds with a 6% After-Tax Yield (Numbers Are in Percentage of Bond Proceeds Assuming a Corporate Taxpayer is in the 35% Marginal Tax Bracket)

Type of Bond	Borrower Pays	Lender Receives	Taxes Paid by Lender	Federal Tax Revenue from Bond	Implicit Subsidy to Borrower
Taxable	9.2	9.2	3.2	+3.2	0.0
Tax-exempt	6.0	6.0	0.0	0.0	3.2
Tax Credit	0.0	9.2[a]	3.2[b]	-6.0[b]	9.2

a. The lender is allowed to reduce its tax liability by the amount of the credit.

b. The federal government receives some additional tax revenue because the credit is included in taxable income. However, the loss in revenue from the credit exceeds the revenue gain producing the negative revenue effect.

One way to think of this alternative subsidy is that financial institutions can be induced to purchase these bonds if they receive the same after-tax return from the tax credit bonds that they would from the tax exemption. The value of the credit must be included in taxable income, but is then used to reduce regular or alternative minimum tax liability. Assuming the taxpayer is subject to the regular corporate income tax, the credit rate should equal the ratio of the purchaser's forgone market interest rate on tax-exempt bonds divided by one minus the corporate tax rate. For example, if the tax-exempt interest rate is 6% and the corporate tax rate is 35%, the credit rate would be equal to 0.06/(1-0.35), or about 9.2%. Thus, a financial institution purchasing a $1,000 tax credit bond would receive a $92 tax credit for each year it holds the bond.

The implicit subsidy is much greater for tax credit bonds than for tax-exempt bonds. All of the interest costs for tax credit bonds are paid by the federal taxpayer. For tax-exempt bonds, the federal taxpayer absorbs only the difference between the taxable and tax-exempt interest rates. For example, if the taxable rate is 9.2% and the tax-exempt rate is 6%, the non-tax credit bond receives a subsidy equal to 3.2 percentage points, the difference between 9.2% and 6%. The tax credit bond receives a subsidy equal to all 9.2 percentage points.

The relationship between three types of bonds, all with the same after-tax yield of 6%, is presented in **Table 8**. The most important column is the last, titled "Implicit Subsidy to Borrower," which is synonymous with the federal revenue *loss* presented in **Table 2** for all outstanding tax-exempt debt. The implicit subsidy is the amount the borrower saves because of favorable federal tax treatment. In the case of tax credit bonds, the subsidy is considerably greater than with traditional tax- exempt bonds.

LEGISLATIVE ISSUES

Current legislative interest focuses on altering the tax treatment of state and local debt to provide even greater financial support for a variety of public projects such as education infrastructure, healthcare facilities, and rapid transit. There are several ways the federal government can increase the federal subsidy to state and local governments that issue tax-exempt bonds for these targeted purposes. One, arbitrage rules could be loosened to allow the state or local government to earn more investment income on unused bond proceeds. Less stringent arbitrage rules may also reduce the compliance burden of some smaller government entities freeing more funds for the project. Two, the federal government can change the rules for private activities that qualify for tax-exempt financing. If more activities qualified to use tax-exempt debt finance by virtue of any proposed rules changes, previous congressional efforts to limit the use of tax-exempt debt for non-governmental projects would be mitigated. Third, Congress could introduce a new type of tax favored instrument, such as tax credit bonds, for a broader range of activities.

In addition to the three options highlighted above, many other methods can be employed to enhance the federal subsidy for state and local government capital formation. The desire to subsidize state and local capital formation, which in many cases may be justified, must be weighed against the federal revenue loss and the potential for misallocation of federal tax revenue.

SUGGESTED READINGS

Ballard, Frederic L., Jr. *ABCs of Arbitrage: Tax Rules for Investment of Bond Proceeds by Municipalities* (Chicago: Urban, State, and Local Government Law Section, American Bar Association, 1992).

Describes and explains arbitrage and the arbitrage tax rules that control state and local investment practices.

Congressional Budget Office. *The Tax-Exempt Financing of Student Loans* (Washington: GPO, August 1986).

Provides a legislative history of student loan bonds, describes the operation of student loan authorities, estimates the costs of student loan bonds, and discusses policy alternatives.

Congressional Budget Office. *Small Issue Industrial Development Bonds* (Washington: GPO, September 1981).

Describes the growth, uses, and effects of small-issue IDBs, and discusses policy alternatives.

U.S. Government Accountability Office. *Home Ownership: Mortgage Bonds Are Costly and Provide Little Assistance to Those in Need.* GAO Report RCED-88- 111, March 1988.

Discusses the structure and operation of mortgage revenue bonds and analyzes whether the bonds are successful in increasing home ownership for the target population of lower-income households.

Hilhouse, Albert M. *Municipal Bonds: A Century of Experience* (New York: Prentice-Hall, 1936).

The classic history of the use and development of municipal bonds from their introduction in the 19th century.

Petersen, John E., and Ronald Forbes. *Innovative Capital Financing* (Chicago: American Planning Association, 1985).

Provides discussion of the numerous variations on tax-exempt bonds that have been developed to raise capital for the state and local sector, such as sale-leasebacks, installment purchase contracts, etc.

Public Securities Association. *Fundamentals of Municipal Bonds* (New York: Public Securities Association, 1987).

Describes the structure and functioning of the state and local debt markets.

U.S. Senate. Committee on the Budget. *Tax Expenditures: Compendium of Background Material on Individual Provisions*. S.Prt. 106-65. 1 06th Congress, 2nd session, December 2000.

Provides description, revenue loss estimate, and economic analysis of the effects of governmental bonds and each major category of private-activity bond.

Zimmerman, Dennis. *The Private Use of Tax-Exempt Bonds: Controlling Public Subsidy of Private Activity* (Washington: The Urban Institute Press, 1991).

Provides institutional background: history, legal framework, and industry characteristics. Provides discussion of tax-exempt bonds as an economic policy tool affecting: intergovernmental fiscal relations, the federal budget deficit, efficient resource allocation, and tax equity. Provides a history and economic analysis of tax-exempt bond legislation from 1968 to 1989.

End Notes

[1] Dennis Zimmerman, "History of Municipal Bonds," in his *The Private Use of Tax-Exempt Bonds: Controlling the Public Subsidy of Private Activity* (Washington, The Urban Institute Press, 1991), pp. 17-27.

[2] The decision about preferred alternatives is critical to estimates of the revenue loss from tax-exempt bonds. An entire range of financial and real assets exists with different yields, risk, and degree of preferential taxation. It is not true that the municipal bond purchaser's preferred alternative is always a taxable bond.

[3] These estimates are derived by summing the revenue loss estimates for each activity listed in the tax expenditures budget. Technically, this is incorrect because each activity's revenue loss is calculated in isolation, and there are interactive effects. Nonetheless, without an estimate of the interactive effects' impact on revenue loss, the summing employed here provides the best available order of magnitude.

[4] Douglas Skarr, California Debt and Investment Advisory Commission, "Auction Rate Securities," *Issue Brief*, Aug. 2004, pp. 2-3.

[5] *The Bond Buyer 2007 Yearbook*, SourceMedia Inc., New York, NY.

[6] Exempt facilities subject to the volume cap are the following: mass commuting facilities, water furnishing, sewage treatment, solid waste disposal, residential rental projects, electric energy or gas furnishing, local district heating or cooling provision, and hazardous waste disposal and 25% of high-speed rail facility bonds. 26 I.R.C. Section 14 1(e), Section 142(a), and 146(g).

[7] This does not mean governmental ownership in the conventional sense. It simply means that lease arrangements for private management and operation of bond-financed facilities must be structured to deny accelerated depreciation benefits to the private operator, lease length must conform to the facility's expected service life, and any sale of the facility to the private operator must be made at fair market value. 26 I.R.C. Section 146(g).

[8] For a more extensive explanation of the tax exempt bond provisions in EGTRRA, see CRS Report RS20932 *Tax-Exempt Bond Provisions in the "Economic Growth and Tax Relief Reconciliation Act of 2001 "*, by Steven Maguire.

[9] See CRS Report RL33154, *The Impact of Hurricane Katrina on the State Budgets of Alabama, Louisiana, and Mississippi*, by Steven Maguire.

[10] The 10-year revenue loss estimates for GOZA 2005 are from the Joint Committee on Taxation, *Estimated Revenue Effects of H.R. 4440, the 'Gulf Opportunity Tax Relief Act of 2005,'* as passed by the House of Representatives and the Senate on Dec. 16, 2005, JCX-89- 05, Dec. 20, 2005.

[11] 26 I.R.C. Section 148(a).

[12] For a more detailed explanation of tax credit bonds or QZABs, see CRS Report RS20606, *Tax Credit Bonds: A Brief Explanation*, by Steven Maguire.

[13] 119 Stat. 594.

[14] 119 Stat. 994.

In: Private Activity, Tax-Exempt and Tax Credit… ISBN: 978-1-61470-227-6
Editor: Fredrick Kjellson

Chapter 4

TAX CREDIT BONDS: OVERVIEW AND ANALYSIS

Steven Maguire

SUMMARY

Almost all state and local governments sell bonds to finance public projects and certain qualified private activities. Most of the bonds issued are tax-exempt bonds because the interest payments are not included in the bondholder's (purchaser's) federal taxable income. In contrast, Tax Credit Bonds (TCBs) are a type of bond that offers the holder or the issuer a federal tax credit instead of interest. This report explains the tax credit mechanism and describes the market for the bonds.

There are a variety of TCBs. Qualified zone academy bonds (QZABs), which were the first tax credit bonds, were introduced as part of the Taxpayer Relief Act of 1997 (P.L. 105-34) and were introduced in 1998. Clean renewable energy bonds (CREBs) were created by the Energy Policy Act of 2005 (P.L. 109-58) and "new" CREBs by the Emergency Economic Stabilization Act of 2008 (P.L. 110-343). Gulf tax credit bonds (GTCBs) were created by the Gulf Opportunity Zone Act of 2005 (P.L. 109-135). Authority to issue GTCBs has expired. Qualified forestry conservation bonds (QFCBs) were created by the Food, Conservation, and Energy Act of 2008 (P.L. 110-246). Qualified energy conservation bonds (QECBs) and Midwest Disaster

Bonds (MWDBs) were created by the Emergency Economic Stabilization Act of 2008 (P.L. 110-343).

The American Recovery and Reinvestment Act of 2009 (P.L. 111-5, ARRA) included several bond provisions that use a tax credit mechanism. Specifically, ARRA created Qualified School Constructions Bonds (QSCBs) and a new type of bond that for the first time allows issuers the option of receiving a federal payment instead of allowing a federal tax exemption on the interest payments. These new bonds, Build America Bonds (BABs) and Recovery Zone Economic Development Bonds (RZEDBs), are also unlike other tax credit bonds in that the interest rate on the bonds is a rate agreed to by the issuer and investor. In contrast, the Secretary of the Treasury sets the credit rate for the other TCBs. The authority to issue BABs and RZEDBs expired after 2010.

Each TCB, with the exception of BABs, is designated for a specific purpose or project. Issuers use the proceeds for public school construction and renovation; clean renewable energy projects; refinancing of outstanding government debt in regions affected by natural disasters; conservation of forest land; investment in energy conservation; and for economic development purposes.

All of the TCBs are temporary tax provisions. The QZAB and QSCB credit rate is set at 100% and the new CREB and QECB credit rate is set at 70% of the interest cost. In contrast, the BAB tax credit rate is 35%. There were several bills introduced in the 111th Congress that would have extended all of the tax credit bond programs including BABs. Only QZABs were extended for the 2011 tax year with $400 million of capacity (P.L. 111-312).

In the FY2012 budget, the Obama Administration has proposed extending the BAB program at a lower direct payment credit rate of 28%. The reduced credit rate is intended to minimize the cost to the Treasury and better approximate the revenue-neutral credit rate. In the 112th Congress, several bills have been introduced to extend and expand a modified version of BABs, including H.R. 11, H.R. 736, H.R. 747, and H.R. 992.

INTRODUCTION

Almost all state and local governments sell bonds to finance public projects and certain qualified private activities. Most of the bonds issued are *tax-exempt* bonds because the interest payments are not included in the bondholder's (purchaser's) federal taxable income. Naturally, interest payments not included in taxable income escape federal income taxation. In contrast, interest payments from other types of bonds, such as corporate bonds, are included in a bondholder's taxable income. Because of the difference in taxability, state and local government tax-exempt bonds—often referred to as municipal bonds—offer a lower pre-tax interest rate than corporate bonds.[1]

Typically, the federal government provides a subsidy for projects that use tax-exempt financing because the interest cost for the issuer is reduced, though the subsidy is variable. For example, on August 7, 2008, the average high-grade taxable corporate bond rate was 5.70%, and the average high-grade municipal bond rate was 4.75%.[2] Without the tax exemption, the issuer would have to pay 0.95% (95 basis points) more for each dollar borrowed (5.70% is 0.95% greater than 4.75%).

The turmoil in financial markets in fall 2008, however, had closed this spread to almost zero. In early December 2008, the municipal bond rate was actually higher than the taxable high-grade corporate bond rate and grew to 74 basis points (corporate bonds were 0.74% higher) by mid- December. This relationship has since reversed. On March 10, 2010, the municipal bond interest rate was 4.91% and the corporate bond rate 5.13% (highly rated AAA bonds).[3]

In contrast to tax-exempt bonds, most tax credit bonds (TCBs) allow either the holder or the issuer to claim a federal tax credit equal to a percentage of the bond's par value (face value) for a limited number of years. This credit rate is set at the current yield on taxable bonds. Issuers of tax credit bonds pay less interest (or no interest in the case of the 100% interest rate tax credit) to bondholders. Thus, TCBs can deliver a larger federal subsidy to the issuer than do municipal bonds.[4]

Currently, there are a variety of TCBs. **Table 1** below lists the existing TCBs and their authorization levels. A more detailed description of each type of bond is provided later in the report. Note that P.L. 110-246, enacted in June of 2008, created Section 54A of the tax code. This section contains many parameters common to all TCBs. This revision of the tax code was intended to "standardize" some of the TCB parameters.

As **Table 1** indicates, the American Recovery and Reinvestment Act of 2009 (P.L. 111-5, ARRA) included several bond provisions that use a tax credit mechanism. Specifically, ARRA created Qualified School Construction Bonds (QSCBs). It also allowed issuers the option of receiving a direct payment from the U.S. Treasury instead of tax-exempt interest payments or tax credits for investors. These new bonds, Build America Bonds (BABs) and Recovery Zone Economic Development Bonds (RZEDBs), are also unlike other tax credit bonds in that the interest rate on the bonds is a rate agreed to by the issuer and bond investor. In contrast, the Treasury Secretary sets the credit rate for the other TCBs based on current market conditions. In short, with BABs and RZEDBs, the two parties in the transaction established the tax credit rate, not the Treasury Secretary. The resulting investor tax credit amount or issuer direct payment is equal to 35% of the interest payment for BABs and 45% for RZEDBs.[5]

Table 1. Authorization Levels of Tax Credit Bonds

Code Section	Bond Program	Authorized Amount	Credit Amount	Expires After	Enacting Legislation
Energy					
54	CREBs I	$1,200,000,000	100%	2009	P.L. 109-58
54C	New CREBs I	800,000,000	70%	2010	P.L. 110-343
54C	New CREBs II	1,600,000,000	70%	2010	P.L. 111-5
54D	QECBs I	800,000,000	70%	no expiration	P.L. 110-343
54D	QECBs II	2,400,000,000	70%	no expiration	P.L. 111-5
General Government, Economic Development and Forest Conservation					
54B	QFCBs	500,000,000	100%	2010	P.L. 110-246[a]
54AA	BABs	no limit	35%[b]	2010	P.L. 111-5
1400N(l)	MWDBs	450,000,000	100%	2009	P.L. 110-343
1400U-2	RZEDBs	10,000,000,000	45%[c]	2010	P.L. 111-5
School Construction					
54E	QZABs I	4,400,000,000	100%	2008	P.L. 105-34
54E	QZABs II	3,200,000,000	100%	2011	P.L. 111-5
54F	QSCBs[d]	22,400,000,000	100%	2010	P.L. 111-5

Source: CRS compilation.

a. P.L. 110-246 is the 2008 "Farm Bill" which was originally signed by the President as P.L. 110-234 on May 22, 2008. Clerical errors in P.L. 110-234 required Congress to pass the revised "Farm Bill" enacted on June 18, 2008. P.L. 110-246 repealed P.L. 110-234.

b. The underlying tax credit rate is market determined, not established by the Secretary of the Treasury as with the other TCBs. The credit is 35% of the market-determined interest rate.

c. The credit amount is determined in the same manner as BABs.

d. QSCBs can be issued in 2011 if capacity were carried over from 2010.

Table 2. Tax Credit Bond Acronyms

Acronym	Type of Bond
BABs	Build America Bonds
CREBs	Clean Renewable Energy Bonds
MWDBs	Midwestern Disaster Bonds
QECBs	Qualified Energy Conservation Bonds
QFCBs	Qualified Forestry Conservation Bonds
QSCBs	Qualified School Construction Bonds
QZABs	Qualified Zone Academy Bonds
RZEDBs	Recovery Zone Economic Development Bonds
TCBs	Tax Credit Bonds

In the 111th Congress, P.L. 111-147 expanded the direct payment option beyond BABs to include issuers of new CREBs, QECBs, QZABs, and QSCBs. The QZAB and QSCB credit rate is set at 100% and the new CREB and QECB credit rate is set at 70% of the interest cost. In contrast, the BAB tax credit rate is 35%. There are several bills in the 112th Congress that would extend BABs. QZABs, however, were extended for the 2011 tax year with $400 million of capacity (P.L. 111- 312).

Each TCB (with the exception of BABs) is designated for a specific purpose or type of project. Issuers of QZABs are required to use the proceeds to finance public school partnership programs in economically distressed areas. CREBs are designated for clean renewable energy projects. MWDB proceeds are for the refinancing of outstanding government debt in regions affected by the Midwestern storms and floods in the spring and summer of 2008. QFCBs are intended to help non-profits or government entities purchase and conserve forest land. QECBs are for investment in capital projects that improve energy conservation. QSCBs are for school construction, BABs are for any governmental purpose, and RZEDBs are for economic development purposes.[6] This report will rely on acronyms to reference the numerous tax credit bonds. **Table 2** summarizes the acronyms for the bonds examined in this report.

THE DETAILS OF TAX CREDIT BONDS

TCBs generally allow the bondholder or issuer to claim a tax credit equal to a specified credit rate as determined by the Secretary of the Treasury for

100% credit rate bonds or by bond counterparties for the other TCBs. The rate of credit is set by the Secretary of Treasury such that the bonds need not be sold at a discount (for a price less than the face value) or with interest costs to the issuer. The Secretary of Treasury does not play a role in setting the credit rate for TCBs that have a credit rate less than 100%. Following is a description of the TCB mechanism.

The Mechanics of TCBs

The method for determining the tax credit rate is generally the same for 100% and 70% credit TCBs.[7] Since July 1999, the Secretary of the Treasury has established a national credit rate that is intended to allow issuers of TCBs to sell their bonds at par (face value) without additional interest expense. The rate calculation is

> based on its [the Treasury Department's] estimate of the yields on outstanding bonds from market sector selected by the Treasury Department in its discretion that have an investment grade rating between A and BBB for bonds of a similar maturity for the business day immediately preceding the sale date of the tax credit bonds.[8]

The credit rate published (by the U.S. Bureau for Public Debt) on the issue sale date is the bondholder's annual rate of credit.

For example, the annual tax credit rate for investor credit TCBs was 5.34% on March 14, 2011 (the term was 15 years).[9] The bonds sold on that day would allow the taxpayer to claim a federal tax credit equal to 5.34% multiplied by the face value of the bond. Thus, a $100,000 bond issued on March 14, 2010, would yield an annual tax credit of $5,340 for the bondholder. However, unlike interest on municipal bonds, which does not create a taxable income stream, the credit amount is included in the bond holder's gross income.[10] The credit is limited to the bondholder's current tax liability; it is "non-refundable." Unused tax credits can be carried over to the succeeding tax year.

The credit was reduced for some TCBs. CREBs and QECBs allow for a credit equal to 70% of the full credit described above. Thus, for these bonds, the investor receives 70% of the annual tax credit described above or $3,738. In contrast, BAB and RZEDB credits are 35% and 45%, respectively, of a market-determined taxable bond interest rate for the specific issuer, not the Secretary of Treasury.

Tax Credit Bonds vs. Other Bonds

The Treasury-determined credit rate for investor credit TCBs is set higher than the municipal bond rate to compensate for the credit's taxability noted earlier. Generally, to attract investors, the credit rate should yield a return greater than the prevailing municipal bond rate and at least equal to the after-tax rate for corporate bonds of similar maturity and risk.

Consider the following example where we assume an average 4.53% interest rate on municipal debt. Investors in the 15% income tax bracket would need a credit rate of at least 5.33% (4.53% divided by (1 - 0.15) is 5.33%) to choose TCBs over municipal bonds. Investors in the 35% bracket would require a credit rate on TCBs of 6.97% (4.53% divided by (1 - 0.35) is 6.97%). Generally, the TCB credit rate would have to exceed the after-tax return on municipal bonds and the after-tax return on taxable bonds of like term to maturity.

TCB issuers may also establish a bond reserve fund (or sinking fund) for the eventual repayment of the bond principal. Generally, IRS rules allow reserve funds to accumulate just enough to repay the bond principal.[11] The sinking fund provision for TCBs significantly reduces the interest cost to the issuer.

The summary below describes how a potential bond investor would begin to evaluate the attractiveness of a tax credit bond relative to two other bond investments. The choice between TCBs (offering a 100% credit) and traditional tax-exempt municipal bonds depends primarily on the bondholder's tax rate. Bondholders in the highest tax bracket find the tax credit relatively less attractive than do bondholders in the lower brackets. However, the tax credit is fixed at the same rate for all buyers. For TCBs that offer a reduced credit rate, such as CREBs and QECBs, the issuer would augment the tax credit with an interest payment or discount pricing.

The choice between a tax credit bond and a taxable corporate bond is not as dependent upon the bondholder's tax bracket. At comparable levels of default risk, TCBs and taxable bonds are equally attractive to purchasers that anticipate tax liability. However, an investor without tax liability that holds a tax credit bond would be allowed to claim a credit for future tax liability or carry forward the credit. For these investors, "stripping" the tax credits from the bond and selling them to an entity with tax liability would be an option. This stripping technique is explained in the next section.

EVALUATING AN INVESTOR TAX CREDIT BOND INVESTMENT

t = income tax rate of bond holder
r^{TCB} = pre-tax rate of TCB credit
r^{muni} = prevailing interest rate on high grade tax-exempt municipal bonds
r^{tax} = prevailing interest rate on high grade taxable bonds

Purchase a TCB if:

$r^{TCB} > r^{muni} /(1-t)$
or
$r^{TCB} > r^{tax}$

To attract investors, the TCB tax credit rate must be greater than (a) alternative tax-exempt municipal bond interest rate divided by one minus the income tax rate, or (b) the prevailing taxable bond rate.

Tax Credit Bond Stripping

The credits on TCBs are "strippable," or the credits can be separated from the underlying bond.[12] Allowing the separation of the credit from the underlying bond improves the attractiveness and marketability of the TCBs to investors and financial intermediaries. Generally, a financial intermediary could buy the TCB, sell the principal to an investor looking for a longer-term investment, and sell the stream of credits to another investor seeking quarterly income. For example, assume a financial intermediary buys the $100,000 TCB presented above. The intermediary sells the right to the principal portion (the $100,000) of the TCB to a pension fund for $90,000 and sells the stream of credits ($1,980 every quarter for 15 years) to another investor for $90,000. The stripping provision makes TCBs more competitive with traditional bonds.

The Term of TCBs

The maximum term (the number of years for which the credit will be paid)

> shall be the term which the Secretary estimates will result in the present value of the obligation to repay the principal on the bond being equal to 50% of the face amount of the bond.[13]

Specifically, the maximum term of the bonds is determined by the prevailing interest rate for municipal debt with a maturity of greater than 10 years. The maximum term on TCBs issued on March 14, 2011, was set at 15 years. Midwest Disaster Bonds (MWDBs) had a maximum term of two years, and the interest rate reflected the shorter term. The Treasury publishes the credit rate and term daily.

Application of Davis-Bacon Labor Standards

ARRA included a provision that requires some of the TCBs to abide by the labor standards as mandated under the Davis-Bacon Act of 1931. Generally, Davis-Bacon requires that contractors pay workers not less than the locally prevailing wage for comparable work. The following bonds are subject to the Davis-Bacon labor standard: new CREBs, QECBs, QZABs, QSCBs, and RZEDBs.

Allocation and Purpose of Tax Credit Bonds

The authority to issue TCBs is usually capped with a national limit or with a state-by-state cap. BABs were the exception. In addition, some of the TCBs include set asides for sub-state governments or other entities. What follows is a brief overview of how and to whom each bond program allocates the authority to issue the bonds.

Qualified Zone Academy Bonds

The limit for QZAB debt was $400 million annually from 1998 through 2008, $1.4 billion for each of 2009 and 2010, and $400 million for 2011.[14] A limit is allocated to each state, the District of Columbia, and territory based upon their portion of the U.S. population below the poverty line. States are responsible for the allocation of the available credit to the local governments or qualified zone academies. Unused credit capacity can be carried forward for up to two years.

Individual public schools use QZABs, through their participating state and local governments, for school renovation (not including new construction), equipment, teacher training, and course materials. To qualify for the program, the school must also be a "Qualified Zone Academy." A "Qualified Zone Academy" is any public school (or program within a public school) that provides and develops educational programs below the postsecondary level if

> such public school or program (as the case may be) is designed in cooperation with business to enhance the academic curriculum, increase graduation and employment rates, and prepare students for the rigors of college and the increasingly complex workforce.[15]

In addition, the academy must also be located in an empowerment zone or enterprise community. Alternatively, the academy also qualifies if it is reasonably expected that at least 35% of the students qualify for the free or reduced price school lunch program. At least 95% of the bond proceeds must be used for rehabilitating or repairing public school facilities, providing equipment, developing course materials, or training teachers and other school personnel.

Qualified School Construction Bonds

These bonds had a national limit of $11 billion in each of 2009 and 2010. An additional $200 million in each of 2009 and 2010 was allocated to Indian schools. The bonds generally are allocated to states based on the state's share of Title 1 Basic Grants (Section 1124 of the Elementary and Secondary Education Act of 1965; 20 U.S.C. 6333, BG). The District of Columbia and the possessions of the U.S. are considered states for QSCBs. The possessions other than Puerto Rico (American Samoa, Commonwealth of the Northern Mariana Islands, Guam, and U.S. Virgin Islands), however, are allocated an amount on the basis of the possession's population with income below the poverty line as a portion of the entire U.S. population with income below the poverty line.

As noted above, 40% of the bond volume ($4.4 billion) is dedicated to large LEAs. A "large" LEA is defined as one of the 100 largest based on the number of "children aged 5 though 17 from families living below the poverty level." Also, one of not more than an additional 25 LEAs can be chosen by the Secretary if the LEA is

> in particular need of assistance, based on a low level of resources for school construction, high level of enrollment growth, or such other factors as the Secretary deems appropriate.[16]

Each large LEA, as defined above, would receive an allocation based on the LEA's share of the total Title I basic grants directed to large LEAs. The state allocation is reduced by the amount dedicated to any large LEAs in the state.

States are currently authorized to issue $3.2 billion of QZABs and were authorized to issue $22 billion of QSCBs. QZAB allocations will be made through 2011 and may be carried forward up to two years. QSCB allocations will also be made through 2010 but can be carried forward indefinitely. On March 14, 2011, the credit rate on QZABs and QSCBs was 5.34% and the term 15 years. As noted earlier, issuers of QZABs and QSCBs can choose the direct payment option before 2011.

Clean Renewable Energy Bonds[17]

As authorized by P.L. 109-58, the original CREBs, which could have been issued through 2009, had a national limit of $1.2 billion of which a maximum of $750 million can be granted to governmental bodies. In addition to governmental bodies, cooperative electric companies and a "clean renewable energy bond lender" can issue the bonds. A clean renewable energy bond lender is defined in the tax code as

> a lender which is a cooperative which is owned by, or has outstanding loans to, 100 or more electric companies and is in existence on February 1, 2002, and shall include any affiliated entity which is controlled by such lender.[18]

The CREB lender would lend to co-ops or governmental bodies. The Secretary of the Treasury reviews applications and selects projects "as the Secretary deems appropriate."[19] Thus, CREBs are not allocated by formula and there are no state minimums. The Internal Revenue Service, through IRS Notice 2005-9 8, described the allocation strategy of the Secretary.[20] The smallest dollar amount projects are considered first and the allocations continue for ever larger dollar amount projects until the entire allocation is consumed.

The term and credit rate for CREBs were determined in the same manner as the other TCBs. These original CREBs offered a 100% credit.

CREBs are available to finance qualified energy production projects which include (1) wind facilities, (2) closed-loop bio-mass facilities, (3) open-loop bio-mass facilities, (4) geothermal or solar energy facilities, (5) small irrigation power facilities, (6) landfill gas facilities, (7) trash combustion facilities, (8) refined coal production facilities, and (9) certain hydropower facilities.

New Clean Renewable Energy Bonds

As originally authorized in P.L. 110-343, the *new* CREBs have a national limit of $2.4 billion to be issued before December 31, 2009. In contrast to the original CREBs, as noted in Table 1, the credit rate on new CREBs is 70% of the credit rate offered on the original CREBs. Not more than one-third of new CREBs may be allocated to any of the following: (1) public power providers, (2) governmental bodies, or (3) projects of cooperative electric companies. For public power providers, the Secretary determines the qualified projects which "are appropriate for receiving an allocation." Each will receive a share of the allocation based on the ratio of the projected cost of the project relative to all other qualified projects receiving an allocation.[21] Governmental bodies and co-ops receive an allocation in an amount the "Secretary determines appropriate."[22] As with original CREBs, there is not a state-by-state minimum or formula allocation mechanism. As noted earlier, issuers of new CREBs can choose the direct payment option.

Qualified Energy Conservation Bonds

QECBs were first created under P.L. 110-343 with a national limit of $800 million.[23] The program was expanded with an additional $2.4 billion under P.L. 111-5 for a total available authority of $3.2 billion. Similar to the new CREBs, these tax credit bonds offer a credit rate that is 70% of the credit rate offered on old CREBs and other TCBs. The authority to allocate QECBs does not expire.

QECBs were allocated to states based on the state's share of total U.S. population. The District of Columbia and the possessions of the U.S. are considered states for QECBs. Large local governments, defined as any municipality or county with population of greater than 100,000, are eligible for a direct allocation. Counties that contain a large city can be eligible if its population less the large city population is still greater than 100,000.

These bonds are to be used for capital expenditures for the purposes of (1) reducing energy consumption in publicly owned buildings by at least 20%; (2) implementing green community programs; (3) rural development involving the production of electricity from renewable energy resources; or (4) programs listed above for CREBs. Also included are expenditures on research facilities and research grants, to support research in (1) development of cellulosic ethanol or other nonfossil fuels; (2) technologies for the capture and sequestration of carbon dioxide produced through the use of fossil fuels; (3) increasing the efficiency of existing technologies for producing nonfossil fuels; (4) automobile battery technologies and other technologies to reduce fossil fuel consumption in transportation; and (5) technologies to reduce energy use in buildings. Energy saving mass commuting facilities and demonstration projects are also included in the list of qualified purposes.

As noted earlier, issuers of QECBs could have chosen the direct payment option.

Forestry Conservation Bonds

QFCBs were limited to $500 million to be allocated before May 22, 2010 (24 months after enactment of P.L. 110-246), in a manner "as the Secretary determines appropriate."[24] Once the bonds are issued, the proceeds must be spent within three years. A unique feature of QFCBs is the allowance for an allocation amount to be used to offset any taxes due the federal government. Any allocation amount used to settle outstanding federal tax debts cannot be used for bond issuance. A qualified issuer is a "State or any political subdivision or instrumentality thereof or a 501 (c)(3) organization."[25]

For purposes of the QFCB program, a qualified forestry conservation purpose must meet the following criteria:[26]

(1) Some portion of the land acquired must be adjacent to United States Forest Service Land.
(2) At least half of the land acquired must be transferred to the United States Forest Service at no net cost to the United States and not more than half of the land acquired may either remain with or be conveyed to a State.
(3) All of the land must be subject to a native fish habitat conservation plan approved by the United States Fish and Wildlife Service.
(4) The amount of acreage acquired must be at least 40,000 acres.

Midwest Disaster Bonds

MWDBs were designated for areas impacted by the severe storms and flooding in the Midwest that occurred between May 1, 2008, and August 1, 2008. Each affected area could have issued an amount based on the population of the affected area. States with over 2 million affected residents were authorized to issue up to $100 million and those with less than 2 million and more than 1 million could have issued $50 million. States with an affected population under 1 million were not eligible to issue MWDBs. Based on IRS guidance, Illinois, Missouri, and Nebraska could have issued up to $50 million each. Indiana, Iowa, and Wisconsin could have issued up to $100 million.[27] These bonds could have been issued in calendar year 2009 only and unlike the other TCBs, had a maximum term of two years. The credit rate on the bonds reflected the relatively short term of the bonds.

The bonds were intended for states to use to help those sub-state jurisdictions which were under fiscal stress. Specifically, the proceeds from MWDBs were to be used to pay the principal and interest on any outstanding state bonds or the bonds of any affected political subdivision within the state. The proceeds could also have been loaned to a jurisdiction for the same purpose. The provision required the issuer to issue an equal amount of general obligations for the same purpose, akin to a matching requirement.

Build America Bonds

BABs were not targeted in their designation as were other TCBs. The volume of BABs was not limited and the purpose was constrained only by the requirement that "the interest on such obligation would (but for this section) be excludible from gross income under section 103."[28] Thus, BABs could have been issued for any purpose that would have been eligible for traditional tax-exempt bond financing other than private activity bonds. The bonds must have been issued before January 1, 2011.

In the 112th Congress, several bills have been introduced to extend and expand a modified version of BABs, including H.R. 11, H.R. 736, H.R. 747, and H.R. 992. **Table 3** summarizes the legislation based on the proposed percent credit rates by year. The percent credit rate on outstanding BABs is 35%.

Table 3. Legislation in the 112th Congress that Would Extend BABs Proposed Percent Credit by Year

Year	H.R. 11	H.R. 736	H.R. 747	H.R. 992
2011	32%	32%	28%	32%
2012	31%	30%	28%	31%
2013	X	30%	X	X
2014	X	30%	X	X

Source: CRS summary based on legislation as introduced.

Notes: All of the proposed extensions would allow for the bonds to be used for current refundings and with the exception of H.R. 747 would include capital expenditures for levees and other flood control projects.

BAB Mechanics

Unlike the other TCBs, the BAB credit amount is 35% of the interest rate established between the buyer and issuer of the bond, not the Secretary of the Treasury. The issuer and investor agree on terms either as a result of a competitive bid process or through a negotiated sale. For example, if the negotiated taxable interest rate is 8%, on $100,000 of bond principal, then the credit is $2,800 (8% times $100,000 times 35%). The issuer has the option of receiving a direct payment from the Treasury equal to the credit amount or allowing the investor to claim the credit. The issuer would choose the direct payment option if the net interest cost was less than traditional tax-exempt debt of like terms. The interest cost to the issuer choosing the direct payment is $8,000 less the $2,800, or $5,200. If the tax-exempt rate is greater than 5.20% (requiring a payment of greater than $5,200), then the direct payment BAB is a better option for the issuer.[29]

As long as the marginal tax rate that clears the municipal bond market is lower than the credit rate on BABs of 35%, then municipal issuers would likely choose the BAB option. However, if the market clearing marginal tax rate rises, the alternative to BABs, traditional tax-exempt bonds, would be relatively more attractive to issuers and investors alike.[30] Increases in statutory marginal tax rates would likely induce such an outcome, reducing the attractiveness of BABs relative to traditional tax-exempt bonds.

A U.S. Treasury Department report on BABs estimated that through March of 2010, the bonds had saved municipal issuers roughly $12 billion in interest costs.[31]

BABs: The New Taxable Bond Option

The BAB, in cases where the issuer claims the direct payment, is modeled after the "taxable bond option," which was first considered in the late 1960s. In 1976, the following was posited by the then president of the Federal Reserve Bank in Boston, Frank E. Morris:

> The taxable bond option is a tool to improve the efficiency of our financial markets and, at the same time, to reduce substantially the element of inequity in our income tax system which stems from tax exemption [on municipal bonds]. It will reduce the interest costs on municipal borrowings, but the benefits will accrue proportionally as much to cities with strong credit ratings as to those with serious financial problems.[32]

The taxable bond option has been well received by issuers and investors. The Securities Industry Financial Markets Association (SIFMA) reports that through 2010, almost $181.4 billion in BABs have been offered.[33]

Recovery Zone Economic Development Bonds

RZEDBs are a special type of BAB. Instead of the 35% credit, RZEDBs offered a 45% credit and are targeted to economically distressed areas. Specifically, these bonds are for any area designated by the issuer (1) as having significant poverty, unemployment, rate of home foreclosures, or general distress; (2) economically distressed by reason of the closure or realignment of a military installation pursuant to the Defense Base Closure and Realignment Act of 1990; or is (3) an empowerment zone or renewal community.[34] The purpose of the bonds is, as the name implies, economic development. Specifically, the bonds are to be used for

> (1) capital expenditures paid or incurred with respect to property located in such zone [recovery zone], (2) expenditures for public infrastructure and construction of public facilities, and (3) expenditures for job training and educational programs.[35]

The volume limit for RZEDBs is $10 billion and is allocated to states (including DC and the possessions) based on the state's employment decline in 2008. All states that experienced an employment decline in 2008 receive an allocation that bares the same ratio as the state's share of the total employment decline in those states. However, all states and U.S. territories, regardless of employment changes, are guaranteed a minimum of 0.90% of the $10 billion.

Large municipalities and counties are also guaranteed a share of the state allocations based on the jurisdiction's share of the aggregate employment decline in the state. A large jurisdiction is defined as one with a population of greater than 100,000. For counties with large municipalities receiving an allocation, the county population is reduced by the municipal population for purposes of the 100,000 threshold. Authority to issue RZEDBs expired January 1, 2011.

In the 112th Congress, H.R. 992 includes an extension of RZEDBs through 2012 with an additional $10 billion in 2011 and $15 billion in 2012. In contrast to the first round of RZEDBs, the proposed extension would allocate bond authority based on each state's share of total unemployment. As with the first round, each state and territory would be guaranteed a minimum of 0.90% of the $25 billion.

End Notes

[1] For ease of exposition, the phrase "state and local tax-exempt bonds" is replaced by "municipal bonds" for the remainder of the report.

[2] Federal Reserve Board, Table H. 15, "Selected Interest Rates," at http://www.federalreserve.gov/releases/H15/ data.htm#top.

[3] Federal Reserve Board, Table H. 15, "Selected Interest Rates," at http://www.federalreserve.gov/releases/H15/ *data*.htm#top, visited June 4, 2010.

[4] See CRS Report RL30638, *Tax-Exempt Bonds: A Description of State and Local Government Debt*, by Steven Maguire.

[5] BABs and RZEDBs where the issuer chooses the direct payment option do not allow for the investor tax credit.

[6] For issuers choosing the direct payment option, the BABs must be used for capital expenditures.

[7] See 26 U.S.C. 54A(b).

[8] U.S. Department of the Treasury, Internal Revenue Service, Internal Revenue Bulletin 2009-6, February 9, 2009, p. 449.

[9] Unlike other TCBs, CREBs have a range of possible maturities (term), but have the same credit rate as the other TCBs of like term.

[10] In special cases, some insurance companies may indirectly pay income tax on otherwise tax exempt debt. In addition, interest paid on private activity bonds may be subject to the alternative minimum tax.

[11] The U.S. Treasury publishes a maximum yield for these reserve funds along with the credit rate. The permitted sinking fund yield is equal to 110% of the long-term adjusted applicable federal rate (AFR), compounded semiannually. The permitted sinking fund yield is updated monthly.

[12] 26 U.S.C. 54A(i).

[13] 26 U.S.C. 54A(d)(5)(B). The term of TCBs is found by calculating the following: $log(2)/log(1+r)$. The variable r is the "discount rate of the average annual interest rate of tax-exempt obligations having a term of 10 years or more which are issued during the month."

[14] According to IRS Notice 2009-30, the $1.4 billion is for each of 2009 and 2010.

[15] 26 U.S.C. 54E(d)(1)(A). The private entity must donate an amount equivalent to 10% of the bond proceeds. Services of employees as volunteer mentors satisfies the 10% private partnership requirement.

[16] 26 U.S.C. 54F(d)(2)(E)(ii). The Secretary did not exercise this option for 2009.

[17] For more on CREBs, see CRS Report R41573, *Tax-Favored Financing for Renewable Energy Resources and Energy Efficiency*, by Molly F. Sherlock and Steven Maguire.

[18] 26 U.S.C. 54(j)(2).

[19] 26 U.S.C. 54(f)(2).

[20] U.S. Department of Treasury, Internal Revenue Service, Internal Revenue Bulletin 2005-52, December 27, 2005, p. 1213.

[21] 26 U.S.C. 54C(c)(3)(A).

[22] 26 U.S.C. 54C(c)(3)(B).

[23] For more on QECBs, see CRS Report R41573, *Tax-Favored Financing for Renewable Energy Resources and Energy Efficiency*, by Molly F. Sherlock and Steven Maguire.

[24] 26 U.S.C. 54B(d)(1).

[25] 26 U.S.C. 54B(f).

[26] 26 U.S.C. 54B(e).

[27] Internal Revenue Service, Internal Revenue Bulletin 2008-50, Notice 2008-109, p. 1285.

[28] 26 U.S.C. 54AA(d)(1)(A). BAB proceeds that use the direct payment options are to be used only for capital expenditures.

[29] Note that if the credit is claimed by the issuer, the transfer to the issuer is an outlay of the federal government, not a tax credit. This simple example does not consider issuance and underwriter fees.

[30] Researchers have determined that the federal government subsidy for BABs "...disadvantages individual U.S. taxpayers, who are the main holders of municipal bonds, and benefits new entrants in the municipal bond market." New entrants would include international investors and pension funds. See Ang, Andrew, Vineer Bhansali, and Yuhan Xing, "Build America Bonds," *National Bureau of Economic Research, Working Paper 16008*, May 2010.

[31] U.S. Treasury Department, "Treasury Analysis of Build America Bonds and Issuer Net Borrowing Costs," April 2, 2010.

[32] Morris, Frank E., "The Taxable Bond Option," *National Tax Journal*, vol. 29, no. 3, September 1976, p. 356.

[33] See http://www.sifma.org/research/research.aspx?ID=12476.

[34] 26 U.S.C. 1400U-1(b).

[35] 26 U.S.C. 1400U-2(c).

CHAPTER SOURCES

Chapter 1 - This is an edited, reformatted and augmented version of a Congressional Research Service publication, RL31457, dated September 10, 2010.

Chapter 2 - This is an edited, reformatted and augmented version of a Congressional Research Service publication, RL34159, dated April 25, 2008.

Chapter 3 - This is an edited, reformatted and augmented version of a Congressional Research Service publication, RL30638, dated March 26, 2008.

Chapter 4 - This is an edited, reformatted and augmented version of a Congressional Research Service publication, R40523, dated March 15, 2011.

INDEX

S

T

U

V

W

Y